Effective Practices in Correctional Settings-II
(Epics-II)

sdg

Effective Practices in Correctional Settings-II
(Epics-II)

Christopher T. Lowenkamp,
Melanie S. Lowenkamp &
Charles R. Robinson

Copyright ©2010, Christopher T. Lowenkamp, Melanie S. Lowenkamp & Charles R. Robinson

For additional information contact M. S. Lowenkamp at mlowenkamp@hotmail.com or 330 391 0100

ISBN 978-1-105-23298-5

Table of Contents

Table of Exercises and Figures vii
Training Expectations ix
Chapter 1: Rationale for Training 1
    Nothing Works? 1
    Some Things Do Work! 3
        Relationship 3
        What we talk about 6
        What other skills are important? 7
    Summary 8
Chapter 2: Relationship & Coaching Skills 11
    Collaboration, Autonomy, Self-efficacy 13
    Empathy 14
    Active Listening 15
    Giving Feedback 18
    Role Clarification 20
    Structured Skill Building and Graduated Practice 23
    Summary 28
Chapter 3: Assessment, Relapse Prevention, and Session Structure 29
    Assessment 29
    Behavioral Analysis 30
        Behavioral Analysis Interview guide 35
    Recognize, Avoid, Cope, Evaluate 43
    Structure of an Interaction 48

    Check-in, Homework, Assess & Apply, Reinforce, Teach 48

    Summary 49

Chapter 4:   Bridging Skills 51

    Stages of Change 51

    Effective Reinforcement 55

    Effective Disapproval 60

    Effective Use of Authority 64

    Summary 67

Chapter 5:   Intervention Skills 69

    Cognitive Model 69

    Applying and Reviewing the Cognitive Model 75

    Problem-Solving Skills 78

    Time-Out 82

    Summary 84

References 85

APPENDIX 95

Table of Exercises and Figures

Exercise 2.1. Active Listening 15
Exercise 2.2. Active Listening Exercise 18
Exercise 2.3. Giving Feedback 20
Exercise 2.4. Role Clarification 22
Exercise 2.5. Structured Skill Building 27
Exercise 3.1. Identifying Risk Factors 30
Exercise 3.2. Behavioral Analysis 33
Figure 3.1. Sample Behavioral Analysis. 34
Exercise 3.3. Behavioral Analysis Role-Play 38
Figure 3.2. Behavioral Analysis Worksheet 39
Exercise 3.4. RACE Role-Play 46
Figure 3.3. Recognize, Avoid, Cope, Evaluate 47
Figure 4.1. Cost-benefit analysis 54
Exercise 4.1. Effective use of reinforcement 58
Exercise 4.2. Effective use of disapproval 63
Exercise 4.3. Effective use of authority 66
Exercise 4.4. When to use disapproval and when to use effective authority 67
Exercise 5.1. Teaching the Cognitive Model 72
Figure 5.1. Pictorial of Cognitive Model 73
Figure 5.2. Pictorial of Cognitive Model with Replacement Thoughts 74
Exercise 5.2. Applying the Cognitive Model 76

Figure 5.3. Completed Worksheet for Exercise 5.2 77
Exercise 5.3. Problem Solving 80
Figure 5.4. Problem Solving Worksheet 81
Exercise 5.5. Time-Out 83
Figure A.1. Behavioral Analysis Worksheet 96
Figure A.2. Recognize, Avoid, Cope, Evaluate 99
Figure A.3. Problem-Solving Worksheet 104
Figure A.4. Time-Out 107
Figure A.5. Self-Assessment Form 110
Figure A.6. Coaching Feedback Form 114
Figure A.7. Cognitive Model 1 119
Figure A.8. Cognitive Model 2 121

Training Expectations

1. Please come prepared to participate.
2. Respect the contributions of your fellow participants.
3. Respect each other while conducting role-plays. This can be a stressful experience for some participants. Please be supportive of one another.
4. Everyone must participate in the facilitated practice exercise.
5. If you finish preparing for your role-play before the preparation time ends, switch roles and continue trying the skill.
6. The facilitated practices will each have three triads. Each triad will be assigned at least one skill.

Each triad will have three roles: observer, offender, and officer. The duties associated with each include:

Observer – monitors the officer's attempt at performing the skill in the triad and gives structured feedback and coaching.

Offender – works with the others in your triad to develop a role-play consistent with the scenario you were given. Vividly play the role of the offender based on the scenario provided. Work with the officer to demonstrate the skill to the other members of your small group. Remember to focus on allowing the officer to try the skill.

Supervision Officer – works with the others in your triad to develop a role-play consistent with the scenario you were given. Practice using the skill assigned in the role-play and be receptive to feedback. Demonstrate the skill for the other members of your small group.

7. Please be sure to ask questions as they arise. Your group facilitator is there to help you with the skill.

Chapter 1

Rationale for Training

Nothing Works?

In 1974 Martinson published a meta-analysis that reviewed the correctional research to date. Martinson concluded that "...with few and isolated exceptions..." not one type of program seemed to have an appreciable effect on recidivism. One of the "programs" reviewed in this analysis was parole. While Martinson and Wilkes[1] later stressed the importance and potential promise in parole supervision (see also Palmer[2]), Martinson's earlier 1974 review[3] failed to find a consistent treatment effect for community supervision.

More than 30 years later, as part of a larger study, Jim Bonta and his colleagues reviewed the research on probation and parole that had been published since Martinson's original article.[4] Bonta et al. came to a conclusion similar to that of Martinson: that the impact of community supervision was limited at best and non-existent in the most pessimistic interpretation.

A recent nearly national study by Solomon, Kachnowski, and Bahti under the auspices of the Urban Institute came to a strikingly

---

[1] Martinson, R., & Wilks, J. (1977). Save parole supervision. *Federal Probation* 41: 23-27.

[2] Palmer, T. (1975). Martinson revisited. *Journal of Research in Crime and Delinquency*, 12: 131-152.

[3] Martinson, R. (1974). What works?—Questions and answers about prison reform. *The Public Interest*, 35: 22-54.

[4] Bonta, J., Rugge, T., Scott, T.-L., Bourgon, G. & Yessine, A. (2008) 'Exploring the black box of community supervision', *Journal of Offender Rehabilitation* 47: 248-270.

similar conclusion: "Overall, parole supervision has little effect on rearrest rates of released prisoners."[5] Further, an annual report released by the State of California indicated that the recidivism rate of its parolees is almost 60 percent, with some counties hitting almost 80 percent.[6]

Finally, a recent study by Green and Winik (2010:375) reviewed the impact of different sentencing options on felony drug offenders.[7] The authors found that, net the effect of other factors, "...the median defendant who experiences both incarceration and probation is expected to recidivate at approximately the same rate as a defendant released without punishment or supervision." That is, recidivism rates of those that went to prison or were placed on probation didn't differ from those that went home!

One of the questions that arises from this literature is: "Should we expect any different outcomes from community supervision?" Anecdotally, we can attest to the fact that officers' caseloads approach 100 in many jurisdictions. One published document is replete with examples of officers having caseloads far exceeding 100 cases.[8] Camp and Camp report that the average caseload in 2001 for probation officers, parole officers, and mixed caseloads was 127, 63, and 84 respectively.[9]

---

[5] Bonta, J. et al. (2008).

[6] California Department of Corrections. (2009). *Corrections moving forward.* Sacramento, CA: Office of Public and Employee Communications.

For other data on recidivism rates of abortion, see Petersilia, J. (1985). Probation and felony offenders. *Federal Probation*, 49:4-9 and Petersilia, J. & Turner, S (1993), Intensive probation and parole. In Michael Tonry (ed.), *Crime and Justice: A Review of Research*, 17:281-335. Chicago: University of Chicago Press.

For recidivism data on inmates release in the US in 1994, see Langan, P.A. & Levin, D.J. (2002). *Recidivism of prisoners released in 1994*. Washington, DC: Bureau of Justice Statistics.

[7] Green, D.P. & Winik, D. (2010). Using random judge assignments to estimate the effects of incarceration and probation on recidivism among drug offenders. *Criminology* 48(2): 375.

[8] DeMichele, M.T. (2007). *Probation and parole's growing caseloads and workload allocation: strategies for managerial decision making.* Lexington, KY: The American Probation & Parole Association.

[9] Camp, C. & G. Camp (2003). *The corrections yearbook, adult corrections 2002.* Middletown, CT: The Criminal Justice Institute, Inc.

Also, informal polls of participants from various trainings reveal that, the typical officer sees those 100 offenders once a month for 5 to 15 minutes at a time. Assuming a 10-minute interaction once a month, we quickly calculate that traditional probation or parole supervision amounts to 2 hours of contact over a one-year period. Given these limitations on time allotted to see an offender and the typical structure of our correctional systems, these visits often amount to a "check-in" for the offender. According to Taxman (2002), if we don't do more than a check-in, we probably cannot rely on community supervision to produce changes in offender outcomes.[10] However, if we can get away from the traditional and standard check-in, community supervision can impact outcomes.

Is Taxman right? Does research exist to support the notion that moving beyond a check-in during probation or parole supervision will impact offender outcomes? YES! Taxman is right! And that is good news for community supervision.

This conclusion leads to another question: What does the research say about being effective in probation and parole? We now turn to this issue.

Some Things Do Work!

Relationship

The most current (and some not so current) research on community supervision indicates that improvements in the effectiveness of community supervision are possible. The research on supervision reveals that the quality or nature of the relationship between the officer and offender has some impact on caseload outcomes.[11] If

---

[10] Taxman, Faye (2002). Supervision—Exploring the dimensions of effectiveness. *Federal Probation* 66(2): 14-27.

[11] Skeem, J., Eno Louden, J., Polasheck, & Cap, J. (2007). Relationship quality in mandated treatment: Blending care with control. *Psychological Assessment*, 19: 397-410.

Paparozzi, M. (1994). *An evaluation of the New Jersey Board of Parole's intensive supervision program*. Doctoral dissertation. Newark, NJ: Rutgers University.

we consider the research in correctional settings in general as relevant to community supervision, then the works of Dowden & Andrews[12] and also Palmer[13] also support the notion that the relationship between an officer and offender is important.

What type of relationship is important? Looking at Skeem et al.,[14] Dowden & Andrews,[15] and Andrews & Kiessling,[16] it appears that a firm but fair and caring relationship produces better results. It is important for correctional staff to adopt a balanced approach in dealing with offenders (see also Paparrozzi & Gendreau,[17] As correctional staff we want to be sure to recognize the "humanity of offenders" but also their "pathology," as described by Cullen.[18]

Paparozzi, M.A. & Gendreau, P. (2005). An intensive supervision program that worked: Service delivery, professional orientation, and organizational supportiveness. *The Prison Journal*, 85(4): 445-466.

[12] Dowden, C. & Andrews, D.A. (2004). The importance of staff practices in delivering effective correctional treatment: A meta-analytic review of core correctional practices. *International Journal of Offender Therapy and Comparative Criminology*, 48: 203-214.

[13] Palmer, T. (1965). Types of treaters and types of juvenile offenders. *Youth Authority Quarterly*, 18: 14-23.

Palmer, T. (1973). Matching worker and client in corrections. *Social Work*, 18: 95-103.

Palmer, T. (1975). Martinson revisited. *Journal of Research in Crime and Delinquency*, 12: 131-152.

Palmer, T. (1991). The effectiveness of intervention: Recent trends and current issues. *Crime and Delinquency*, 37: 330-346.

Palmer, T. (1994). *A profile of correctional effectiveness and new directions for research*. Albany, NY: SUNY Press.

Palmer, T. (1995). Programmatic and nonprogrammatic aspects of successful intervention: New directions for research. *Crime and Delinquency*, 41: 100-131.

[14] Skeem et al. (2007).

[15] Dowden & Andrews (2004).

[16] Andrews, D.A. & Kiessling, J.J. (1980). Program structure and effective correctional practices. A summary of CaVIC research. (pp. 441-463). In R.R. Ross & P. Gendreau (Eds.), *Effective correctional treatment*. Toronto: Butterworths.

[17] Paparozzi & Gendreau (2005).

[18] Cullen, F.T. (2011). Taking rehabilitation seriously: Creativity, science, and the challenge of offender change. *Punishment and Society* (forthcoming).

What does Cullen mean by stating that we sometimes deny the humanity and pathology of offenders? Cullen is illustrating the fact that offenders are similar to us in some ways (their humanity refers to those common characteristics associated with being human, such as having basic needs and the capacity to learn and change) but differ from us in others (at some level offenders find their antisocial behavior functional). Because we do differ from offenders in some ways, the traditional therapeutic relationship needs to be modified to include a more structured and directive interaction. The necessity for this type of quality relationship may seem counterintuitive upon first thought, but it makes considerable sense once the idea is fully understood.[19]

We know the officer-offender relationship is important; however, as Spiegler and Guevremont note, "the relationship is necessary but not sufficient to bring about behavioral change."[20] Aside from paying attention to the relationship we develop with clients, what else can we do to increase our effectiveness? Along with creating a positive working relationship, what we discuss with offenders matters.

---

[19] The following provide discussions and research on the importance of how staff relate to clients in achieving outcomes:

Andrews, D.A. (1999). Assessing program elements for risk reduction: The correctional program assessment inventory. In Patricia M. Harris (Ed.). *Research to results: Effective community corrections.* (pp. 151-170). Lanham, MD: American Correctional Association.

Andrews, D.A., Kiessling, J.J., Russell, R.J. & Grant, B.A. (1979) *Volunteers and the one to one supervision of adult probationers.* Toronto: Ontario Ministry of Correctional Services.

Gendreau, P. (1996). The principles of effective interventions with offenders. In Alan T. Harland (Ed.), *Choosing correctional options that work: Defining the demand and evaluating the supply*: 117-130. Thousand Oaks, CA: Sage.

Gendreau, P. & Andrews, D.A. (1994). *The correctional program assessment inventory.* Saint John, Canada: University of New Brunswick.

Gendreau, P. & Andrews, D. A. (2002). *The correctional program assessment inventory 2000.* (CPAI 2000). Saint John, Canada: University of New Brunswick.

Nesovic, A. (2003). *Psychometric evaluation of the correctional program assessment inventory (CPAI).* Carleton University: Doctoral Dissertation.

[20] Spiegler, M. D., & Guevremont, D. C. (2003). *Contemporary behavior therapy* (4th ed.). Pacific Grove, CA: Wadsworth.

What we talk about

According to Dowden and Andrews and others,[21] what we talk about or "target" with offenders should be their criminogenic needs. Criminogenic needs are things like maladaptive thoughts, skill deficits, unemployment, poor family relationships, and substance abuse.[22] These factors have been shown to impact recidivism again and again.

Further, research on targeting these needs in group settings[23] and one-on-one interactions[24] has shown promise. More specifically, and germane to this training, research by Bonta et al.[25] and Bonta, Rugge, Sedo, and Coles[26] revealed that targeting one or two of these needs led to reductions in recidivism, while targeting compliance-related issues only or targeting multiple criminogenic needs was associated with increases in recidivism. Further, in 2010 Bonta et al. indicated that of all the possible areas, targeting offenders' cognitions in one-

---

[21] Dowden, C. & Andrews, D. A. (1999a). What works for female offenders: A meta-analytic review. *Crime and Delinquency*, 45: 438-452.

Dowden, C. & Andrews, D. A. (1999b). What works in young offender treatment: A meta-analysis. *Forum on Corrections Research*, 11: 21-24.

Gendreau, P., Little, T., & Goggin, C. (1996). A meta-analysis of the predictors of adult offender recidivism: What works! *Criminology*, 34: 575-607.

Jones-Hubbard, Dana and Travis C. Pratt. (2002). A meta-analysis of the predictors of delinquency among girls. *Journal of Offender Rehabilitation*, 34(3):1-13.

Andrews, D. A., & Bonta, J. (2003). *The psychology of criminal conduct* (3rd ed.). Cincinnati, OH: Anderson.

[22] Andrews, D.A., Zinger, I., Hoge, R., Bonta, J., Gendreau, P. & Cullen, F. (1990) Does correctional treatment work? A clinically relevant and psychologically informed meta-analysis. *Criminology* 28 (3): 369-401.

Andrews, D.A. & Bonta, J. (2003). The psychology of criminal conduct 3rd edition. Cincinnati, OH: Anderson Publishing Co.

[23] Dowden, C. & Andrews, D.A. (1999a). What works for female offenders: A meta-analytic review. *Crime and Delinquency*, 45: 438-452.

Dowden & Andrews (1999b).

[24] Bonta et al. (2008).

[25] Bonta et al. (2008).

[26] Bonta, J., Rugge, T., Sedo, B., & Coles, R. (2004). *Case management in Manitoba probation*. Public Safety and Emergency Preparedness, Canada.

on-one interactions with officers was most effective in reducing recidivism.[27] Similarly, Taxman (2008) found that an officer stressing desistance during one-on-one interactions with offenders was associated with reductions in recidivism.[28]

What other skills are important?

Research by published by a variety of authors indicates that several skills, known as core correctional practices, are related to correctional effectiveness.[29] In a systematic review of the existing research, Dowden and Andrews indicate that reinforcement, disapproval, effective use of authority, teaching problem-solving skills, coaching skills, and the use of structured skill building were all related to correctional effectiveness.[30] Brokerage and referral, traditionally used in community supervision, were found to be the least effective of the core correctional practices. While much of the research reviewed by Dowden & Andrews focused on treatment programs in correctional settings, some research has specifically tested the applicability of these skills to community supervision.[31]

---

[27] Bonta, J., Bourgon, G., Rugge, T., Scott, T., Yessine, A.K., Gutierrez, L., & Li, J. (2010). *The strategic training initiative in community supervision: Risk-need-responsivity in the real world*. Ottawa, ON: Public Safety.

[28] Taxman, F.S. (2008). No illusion, offender and organizational change in Maryland's proactive community supervision model. *Criminology and Public Policy*, 7(2): 275-302.

[29] Dowden & Andrews (2004).

Andrews & Kiessling (1980).

Gendreau & Andrews (2002).

Trotter, C. (1996) The impact of different supervision practices in community corrections. *Australian and New Zealand Journal of Criminology* 29(1): 29-46.

Taxman (2008).

[30] Dowden, C. Antonowicz, D., & Andrews, D.A. (2003). The effectiveness of relapse prevention with offenders: A meta-analysis. *International Journal of Offender Therapy and Comparative Criminology*, 47:516-528.

[31] Trotter (1996).

Trotter, C. (1999). *Working with involuntary clients: A guide to practice*. Thousand Oaks, CA: Sage Publications.

Bonta et al. (2008).

Taxman (2008).

Additional research by Taxman[32] and Trotter[33] has shown increased effectiveness in supervision when officers use reinforcement. Trotter's research (1996) further found that the officer's modeling of prosocial behaviors is also associated with reduced recidivism. Finally, a recent study investigating a precursor to EPICS II, indicated that the use of these skills was associated with a reduction in recidivism of 50 percent (relative risk reduction) with moderate risk offenders and a 50 percent relative risk reduction with high-risk offenders when additional training on communication and motivational enhancement was provided).[34]

Summary

What we have traditionally done in corrections in general and community supervision specifically doesn't seem to have strong effects on recidivism. When we think about the research on correctional treatment and supervision, it should not be a big surprise that a system set up to ensure short-term compliance and/or administer punishment falls short in bringing about long-term behavioral change.

The good news is that current research has begun to indicate that what we do and how we do it does in fact hold promise for longer-term reductions in recidivism. Making these changes in our system will not be easy. And the changes, once in place, do not make our work easier than what we do now, but they do make our jobs more challenging, more fulfilling, and more effective. We have seen these comments emerge from focus groups of officers and other correctional practitioners following this training.

We can set about having a greater impact by paying attention to the working relationship that we develop with offenders and also the things we discuss with offenders. More specifically, if we teach

---

[32] Taxman (2008).

[33] Trotter (1996).

[34] Robinson, C.R, VanBenshoten, S., Alexander, M., & Lowenkamp, C.T. (2011). A random (almost) study of Staff Training Aimed at Reducing Rearrest (STARR): Reducing recidivism through intentional design. Federal Probation, 75(2): 57-63.

offenders new skills and behaviors throughout the correctional experience, we should be able to reduce risk. The key to achieving better results is for us to actually learn and use the skills to help offenders change. That is what this training is all about, giving officers an additional skill set that focuses on bringing about longer-term change in offenders. Before we begin discussing and learning the various skills referenced above we are going to spend some time discussing the collection of information through assessment and behavioral analysis, how to use that information to draw up a "strategic plan," and a interaction structure to follow when meeting with clients.

Please note that throughout this document we use the words offender, client, and involuntary client interchangeably. We do recognize that these different terms reflect perceived and real differences; however, within the limited context of this document, consider them to have the same meaning. In an effort to keep the document gender neutral, we have alternated using he and she in examples and exercises.

Chapter 2
Relationship & Coaching Skills

Nothing seems to make a probation or parole officer cringe faster than the use of the "R" word. Yes, based on the seemingly automatic spasms alone, one would think that "relationship" is a dirty word. We want to emphasize that all of the authors have worked with offenders in varying capacities (probation, parole, jail, law enforcement, treatment). While we are all interested in seeing clients change their lives, we recognize that their interaction with you is usually involuntary. Because of this fact, we want to make sure that you understand what we mean when we use the term relationship. We like the Dictionary.com online definition of relationship: "a connection, association, or involvement." Your involvement, association, or connection should be strictly professional and work related. While you want to be friendly (not hostile or at variance, but amicable), you do not want to be friends (a person attached to another by feelings of affection or personal regard). This might seem like a lot of definitions and a lot of attention to such a simple word, but the relationship you build with offenders will be very important. It is analogous to the foundation of a house. If you build a great house on a poor foundation, you will eventually have troubles. A relationship is insufficient, by itself, to bring about change, just as a foundation doesn't make a complete house. However, a working relationship is a necessary foundation to bring about change. Why is this the case?

If you recall your own experiences, what someone thinks about you or your behavior takes on different levels of impact depending upon your relationship with that person. If someone you dislike tells you that he disapproves of something you have done, that will probably have little impact on your behavior; if you are particularly defiant, it might even cause you to increase the use of that behavior. On the other hand, if someone you respect and care about and who clearly respects and cares about you dislikes something you have done, that same disapproval takes on a completely different meaning. A relationship provides us with the avenue to bring about changes. For this reason the relationship is necessary! Below are a number of very basic skills that will assist in developing a working relationship with involuntary clients. Remember that the goal is not to be friends but to be friendly in your interactions.

This notion of developing a quality working relationship isn't just a nice idea. Researchers have identified relationship[35] and coaching skills[36] of staff as important factors associated with effective correctional programs. Meta-analytic results by Dowden & Andrews show that correctional programs with staff that possess relationship and coaching skills are considerably more effective in reducing recidivism than correctional programs with staff that do not possess these skills.[37]

Before we continue it is important to briefly discuss the concept of Motivational Interviewing (MI) and how MI's key components can help to enhance effective relationships with our clients. MI is an evidence-based approach to uncover and resolve the ambivalence preventing a client from making the desired changes in his life.[38] By resolving the client's ambivalence, the officer can assist in increasing his intrinsic motivation for making necessary changes, rather than simply imposing external changes.[39] Therapists in various settings for over 50 years have utilized the

---

[35] Skeem et al. (2007).

Andrews et al. (1990).

Palmer (1965).

Palmer (1973).

Palmer (1995).

[36] Trotter (1996).

Andrews et al. (1990).

[37] Dowden & Andrews (2004).

[38] Miller, W. R., & Rollnick, S. (2002). *Motivational interviewing: Preparing people for change*. New York: Guilford Press.

[39] Miller & Rollnick (2002)

motivational interviewing style with a wide range of problem behaviors. William Miller was the first to use the approach in treating problem drinkers.[40] Many of the same principles used in motivational interviewing are important in successfully implementing the skills contained in the EPICS II curriculum because many high-risk offenders often lack motivation or present as ambivalent about change. Specifically, EPICS II and MI share several key concepts that help to develop trust, rapport and relationships with the clients: collaboration, autonomy, self efficacy, empathy, and active listening.

Some additional skills covered in this chapter include: giving feedback, role clarification, and structured skill building.

Collaboration, Autonomy, Self-efficacy

Three important concepts for developing an effective relationship to promote behavioral change include collaboration, autonomy, and self-efficacy. Collaboration involves creating a non-judgmental partnership with the client that is conducive to change but not coercive. While this partnership is designed to be a two-way interaction it is centered on the client's thoughts and experiences. Collaboration provides a favorable climate to explore the consequences of behavior and offer support for client-driven alternatives, rather than through persuasion or confrontation. Achieving this type of environment requires the avoidance of an "expert-recipient" stance or "lecture-style" approach and instead respects the autonomy, and encourages the self-efficacy, of the client. The client is ultimately responsible for making any behavioral changes. While it is the responsibility of the officer to enforce the rules of the court by meting out the consequences of the client's choices, lasting behavioral changes will be realized when brought about by the client's own intrinsic motivation. The officer can assist in the process by drawing out the client's internal motivation to change and providing the necessary skills to implement the change. By using this method the officer avoids the

---

[40] Miller, W. R. (1983). Motivational interviewing with problem drinkers. Behavioural Psychotherapy, 11, 147-172.

natural tendency to "fix" the client by solving the client's problems and the client becomes engaged and empowered in the search for change and maintains his ability to choose and carry out his behavior.[41] The client is permitted ownership of his choices and is therefore responsible for the outcome. "If the [officer] takes responsibility for the change argument and says 'you need to change and here's how you do it' fairly predictably the client will give you the other side of the argument."[42] Honoring the autonomy of the client allows him to establish reasons for change that are more congruent with his personal values and goals. Furthering those choices by supporting the client's belief in her ability to carry out the change (self-efficacy), the officer is able to increase the likelihood that the client will put the plan into action.[43] Unlike self-esteem, self-efficacy is a person's belief about his or her capability to perform at a certain level and exercise influence over events.[44] Self-efficacy, unlike self-esteem, is found to be a predictor of criminal behavior.[45]

Empathy

Empathy is the ability to identify, understand, and be sensitive to another's thoughts, emotions, or experiences. It is important in building a foundational relationship with the client that the officer communicate an attitude of understanding. Communication must be genuine and non-judgmental. Clients need to feel listened to, understood, and safe in sharing information with their officer and exploring alternatives to their anti-social behavior. By collecting

---

[41] Miller & Rollnick (2002)

[42] Quote from Miller interview on Motivationalinterview.org

[43] Lopez-Viets, V., Walker, D.D., & Miller, W.R. (2002). What is motivation to change? A scientific analysis. In M. McMurran (Ed.), *Motivating Offenders to change: A guide to enhancing engagement in therapy*. Chichester, UK: John Wiley & Sons Ltd.

[44] Bandura, A. (1994). Self-efficacy. In V. S. Ramachaudran (Ed.), *Encyclopedia of human behavior* (Vol. 4, pp. 71-81). New York: Academic Press. (Reprinted in H. Friedman [Ed.], Encyclopedia of mental health. San Diego: Academic Press, 1998).

[45] Andrews & Bonta (2003).

information about a client and responding with empathy the officer has a more in-depth understanding of the thoughts and emotions driving the behavior. As a note of caution, expressing empathy with the client does not mean we necessarily agree with or support the poor behavior. In fact, Chris Trotter's research indicates that the use of empathy without core correctional practices leads to increased failure rates.[46] Empathy can be demonstrated either by verbally acknowledging the other person's emotions or through non-verbal communication, such as facial expressions or a head nodding. An important skill utilized in conveying empathy and understanding is active listening.[47]

Active Listening

Active listening is often misunderstood as a term for simply being polite in communication. However, active listening is a very important skill that is rather engaging and involved. Without active listening real communication cannot occur.[48] Why? Before we begin to discuss what exactly active listening entails, let's first discuss the why. Take a few minutes to complete exercise 2.1 below.

> **Exercise 2.1. Active Listening**
>
> Discuss with those around you why it might be important to use active listening when interacting with clients on your caseload. What message does active listening send to the speaker?

We have discussed the message that active listening sends and why it facilitates open and productive interactions with offenders. The ***steps of active listening*** are listed below. Remember that the goal of active listening is to understand what the individual is communicating in terms of fact, emotion, and thought.

---

[46] Trotter (1996).
[47] Rogers, C., (1961). *On becoming a person*. Boston: Houghton Mifflin.
Gordon, T. (1970). Parent Effectiveness Training. New York: Peter H. Wyden.
[48] Rogers (1961); Gordon (1970).

1. Listen to the whole message.

It is important to let people get the entire story or message out. That way you can process all that they have to say and understand exactly what happened. If you don't listen to the whole message, you might be advising, teaching, correcting, approving, or disapproving when you shouldn't be. Furthermore, interrupting people for any reason is a roadblock to communication.

2. Check for understanding.

Spoken language, while powerful, is a great source of misunderstanding, especially in stressful situations. A valuable tool used to clarify your understanding of the information that is being relayed to you is the acronym OARS from the MI literature.[49] OARS stands for **Open Ended Questions, Affirmations, Reflections, and Summaries.**

Open-ended questions are those that are not easily answered with a "yes" or a "no" or other quick answer. Open-ended questions encourage the speaker to examine the issue more deeply and provide more in-depth information. An example of an open-ended question is "how will receiving your GED help you reach your goals?"

Affirmations are statements that recognize the client's strengths and acknowledge efforts leading to positive change. These affirming statements support self-efficacy by building the client's confidence in their ability to change. Several examples of affirmations are "that's a really good suggestion," "you've accomplished a lot since you started treatment," or "you handled yourself very well in that difficult situation."

Reflective listening is an essential skill in checking for understanding. It is a statement that clarifies understanding on the part of the officer, but from the perspective of the client. The purpose of reflective listening is: to avoid the roadblocks or distractions that interfere change (arguing, blaming,

---

[49] Miller & Rollnick (2002).

warning, or shaming); to ensure that misinterpretation of the material did not occur; and to reflect back to the client the negatives associated with the status quo and positives associated with making changes. Reflective listening may involve repeating, rephrasing or paraphrasing. Some standard phrases that can be used include: "so what I'm hearing you say is...," "it sounds like you...," or "correct me if I'm wrong...."

Summaries are a specific type of reflection where the officer recaps important elements of the conversation. Summaries can be used throughout the conversation, at major transition points or at the end to ensure that the listener is on track with the meaning of the message. To summarize begin with a statement indicating that you are making a summary. For example, "let me see if I understand the situation...," "so, just to recap...," or "let me summarize to make sure I haven't missed anything."[50]

3. Pay attention to non-verbal cues.

Make sure that the non-verbal cues you send communicate your interest in what the offender is saying. Be sure to maintain eye contact and limit distractions such as interruptions from other staff, answering the phone, and entering information into the computer. Also pay attention to the non-verbal cues of the offender, as they can communicate information for reflection or summarization (for example, an offender may articulate that he will go to treatment, but in a way that shows he is clearly uncomfortable).

---

[50] Miller & Rollnick (2002).

> **Exercise 2.2. Active Listening Exercise**
>
> In groups of three, take the roles of offender, officer, and observer.
>
> The *offender* should come into the office to discuss the fact that he or she has failed to show up to treatment and really doesn't feel like going, as it interferes with his or her ability to get to work on time and cuts in on time with family.
>
> The *officer* should:
> 1. Listen to the whole message.
> 2. Check for understanding by asking questions, summarizing, and reflecting.
> 3. Pay attention to non-verbal cues.
>
> The *observer* should pay attention to the interaction to make sure the skill steps are followed by the officer and then go through the process of providing feedback.
>
> Observer notes & feedback:

Giving Feedback

Given the nature of your employment, you will have to give corrective feedback to the offenders you supervise. You will certainly have to give feedback as you work through the RACE document and evaluate how the client has done in applying avoidance and coping skills. You will also, in general, have to give feedback to clients about other various behaviors. How you give feedback matters. Think of the last time you heard someone say to you in a disapproving tone, "Can I give you some advice?" What thoughts did you have when you heard that statement? Given your prior experiences with receiving advice and feedback, you probably had negative thoughts. While your thoughts about this phrase are in part affected by the one who is trying to give you advice (remember the importance of relationship), a part of what you think about the statement is surely shaped by your past experiences in receiving feedback.

There is a way to give feedback that is much more productive and constructive than the informal way we usually do. In general, feedback should be immediate, frequent, and positive. Feedback can always be positive by placing an emphasis on improvement and success. According to research, positive feedback is seen as a rewarding experience,[51] which means that the receiver will become more and more open to receiving feedback in the future. The steps to giving feedback listed below are adapted from Hadfield-Law and focus on giving feedback in a positive and constructive way.[52]

1. Ask the recipient if she is ready for feedback.

Be respectful here, remembering to emphasize personal choice and control. A person may not want to hear feedback for a number of reasons. If the person says no, you may have to wait until some other time. Forcing the feedback might build resentment, inclining the person to ignore it or even to act contrary to it.

2. Ask the recipient what things she did well.

Remember that most people want to go right to what they did wrong and how they might improve. Be sure to keep the person focused on what she did right. If she starts to drift towards what she did wrong or what needs correcting, stop her and tell her that she will have a chance to talk about areas for improvement, but right now you want to focus on what was done well.

3. Tell the recipient what she did well.

Be sure to be behaviorally specific in identifying areas where the individual performed well. Give plenty of recognition and praise during this step. Providing recognition and praise will encourage the use of the behavior in the future.

---

[51] Van Houten, Ron (1998). *How to motivate others through feedback*, 2nd edition. Austin, TX: Pro-Ed, Inc.

[52] Hadfield-Law, L. (2002). *Train your team yourself: How to design & deliver effective in-house training courses*. Oxford, U.K.: How To Books Ltd.

4. Ask the recipient *what she did that needs improvement.*

This might make your job of giving constructive or corrective feedback easier, as people often are their own harshest critics. Do not agree or disagree with her at this point. You will give corrective feedback in step 5. This is the individual's opportunity to think about and articulate what she could have done better.

5. Tell the recipient what you observed that she did that needs improvement.

Be sure to be specific and clear about what needed improvement AND be sure to tell her, in direct and behaviorally specific terms, how to improve her performance in the future.

6. Check for the recipient's understanding, summarize corrective strategies, and then end with what was done correctly.

Notice that this is a "sandwich" method, with the corrective suggestions sandwiched in between positive statements about what the individual did well and your positive summative statement that ends with what was done correctly. This method should make the feedback more encouraging than ending on a corrective note.

Exercise 2.3. Giving Feedback

Watch the modeling of this skill by the facilitators. Keep track of the skill steps and take notes of the process below. You will be using this skill throughout the training and also with offenders after the training.

Role Clarification

Chris Trotter discusses the importance of role clarification when working with involuntary clients. Trotter specifically states that role clarification is identified by the research as a key skill in working with involuntary clients.[53] Role clarification helps the offender understand what you (the officer) are there for and what offenders can expect from you and the process of supervision. Role clarification also gives the offender an understanding of what is expected from him and sets the stage for supervision to be a collaborative process. Role clarification should be covered at the beginning of supervision, but is considered an ongoing process that is more clearly specified and discussed as supervision proceeds.[54]

The steps of role clarification are as follows:

1. Identify the agency's goals for the supervision process.

Typically the agency is interested in protecting the community and helping the offender make changes so that he doesn't end up back in the system (reductions in recidivism).

2. Ask the offender to identify what he hopes to accomplish during the supervision process.

This step is important, as it allows the offender to have some input into the process. The offender's goals might be general (I want a job or I want to get clean) or specific (I want to get a job at ABC and work full time). Either way these goals can be used during case planning.

3. Identify what you, as a representative of the agency, hope to accomplish.

You might explain that your role is to provide services to help offenders comply with the requirements of the court or paroling authority and to support the development of skills to promote change.

---

[53] Trotter (1999): 47-65.

[54] Rooney, R.H. (1992). *Strategies for work with involuntary clients*. New York, NY: Columbia University Press. This work also discusses the importance of role clarification in both individual and group settings although he does not refer to the process as role clarification.

4. Define the supervision process.

In this section you should discuss what is required as part of supervision, what can and cannot be negotiated, and the roles of the offender, officer, judge, and treatment provider (when appropriate). Roles might look like the following:

Offender – Comply with the orders of the court or paroling authority, attend and participate in programming, and apply the skills learned.

Officer – Support skill development, monitor application, and make reports to the court.

Court or Paroling Authority – Review the application of skills and make decisions regarding supervision status.

Treatment provider (if appropriate) – Provide skills needed for compliance and change.

5. Identify and discuss the expectations of confidentiality.

Offenders might be worried about what you will discuss and with whom. It is a good idea to have a frank discussion about this, including what information can/will be shared and the circumstances and purpose for sharing such information.

Exercise 2.4. Role Clarification

In groups of three, take the roles of offender, officer, and observer.

The *offender* reports to the office for an initial visit.

The *officer* should:

1. Identify the district's goals for the supervision process.
2. Ask the offender to identify what he hopes to accomplish during the supervision process.
3. Identify what you (the officer), as a representative of the agency, hope to accomplish.
4. Define the supervision process.
5. Identify and discuss the expectations of confidentiality.

The *observer* should pay attention to the interaction to make sure the officer follows the skill steps and then go through the process

of providing feedback. Observer notes & feedback:

Structured Skill Building and Graduated Practice

Throughout the course of supervision you will most likely recognize that some of the skills required for implementing the recommended behavioral changes are not skills that the client currently possesses. As the officer and client create relapse prevention plans (covered in Chapter 3) the officer must determine what skills are necessary to execute the plan and assess both the client's knowledge of the skills and ability to perform those skills. Often, the client will erroneously equate knowing about the skill with having the skill.[55] Many of the skills you will be teaching/coaching clients to use are new to them. While some may appear to be common sense, it is best not to assume the offender is skilled in using them. Other skills may not be common sense to even non-offending pro-social individuals, so they can be completely foreign to offending anti-social individuals. To ensure that clients understand and learn the skills being taught, the officer should follow a structured skill-building model. To teach them how to use the skills in their high-risk situations (to avoid or manage risk), clients should be given graduated practice opportunities.[56]

---

[55] Lopez-Viets et al. (2002).
[56] Andrews and Kiessling (1980).
Andrews and Gendreau (1990 & 2000).
Andrews and Dowden (2004).
Andrews and Bonta (2003).
Masters, J. C., Burish, T.G., Hollon, S.D., & Rimm, D.C. (1987). *Behavior therapy techniques & empirical findings*, 3rd edition. San Diego, CA: Harcourt Brace Jovanovich, Publishers.

If you draw on your own experiences, you will likely agree that you acquire new behaviors when you are motivated to do so. Further, you are likely to pick up a new behavior more readily if it is described to you in behaviorally specific terms and demonstrated for you. The road to mastering the behavior involves the opportunity to practice the new behavior in fairly "safe" environments, with feedback from someone who knows the behavior well. Finally, individuals should be given the opportunity to use the newly learned skills in increasingly difficult situations.[57]

For example, if you have successfully taught a child to hit a ball with a bat, you have probably used this process. First, for one reason or another, the child was motivated to learn the skill. Perhaps she was graduating from T-ball to a coach-pitch baseball league. Regardless, once the child expressed interest or you had built that interest, the second step in the process was to provide some instruction on how to hold the bat and swing it. Most likely, you demonstrated the skill of holding and swinging the bat. Next you had the child give a few swings and corrected her hold on the bat and where she was standing in relation to the plate. Then you actually began pitching the ball to the child. When you first started pitching the ball, did you throw overhand 100 mph fastballs? No, you threw underhanded lobs so that the child could work on connecting the bat with the ball. All the while you were giving corrective feedback such as "start your swing earlier," "keep your eye on the ball," and so on. As the child mastered the skill of swinging and connecting with the underhand lob, you began throwing overhand pitches that were relatively slow. When the child gained comfort in hitting slow overhand pitches, you picked up the speed. The child then tested her skill in a real game. Afterwards, you or the coach gave the child feedback about what she did well and how she could improve her hitting for the next

---

[57] Goldstein, A.P. (1988). *The prepare curriculum teaching prosocial competencies*. Champaign, IL: Research Press.

Striefel, S. (1998). *How to teach through modeling and imitation*, 2nd edition. Austin, TX: Pro-Ed, Inc.

Panyan, M.V. (1998). *How to teach social skills*, 2nd edition. Austin, TX: Pro-Ed, Inc.

Andrews & Bonta (2003).

game. She then got a chance to work on those deficiencies with you in the backyard or with her coach during scheduled practice.

The analogy for a client might be learning to respond to someone who is angry. First, you have to make sure the client is motivated to learn the skill. Perhaps he has expressed concerns about his ability to deal with people when they yell at him. This skill you are going to teach him is a potential solution to his concern. With the client motivated to learn the skill, you would teach the client the skill steps in a non-threatening environment (e.g., your office or in a group). You might also pick a non-threatening scenario, such as asking the client to respond to a friend that is angry at a third person. Once he masters the skill in this fairly non-threatening situation and context, you would increase the difficulty of the scenario. The second step might involve transferring the skill to responding to a friend when the friend is expressing anger at your client. After successfully completing the second step, a possible third iteration of application would be increasing the complexity and difficulty of the situation by transferring the skill to responding to his wife when she is angry at the offender. The offender should be given the opportunity to practice each of these scenarios using role-play or other behavioral rehearsal techniques. In this scenario the situation has increased in difficulty, reaching the point where it could potentially help your client cope with a high-risk situation (if he does in fact have a hard time dealing with his wife in a prosocial and adaptive way when she is angry with him).

The following steps to teach an offender a new skill are based on the writings of multiple authors[58]:

1. Make sure the client has been motivated to learn the new skill.

If someone doesn't understand the purpose of a skill or see the need for it, that person is not likely to learn or use the

---

[58] Masters et al. (1979).
Striefel (1998).
Panyan (1998).
Andrews & Bonta (2003).
Goldstein (1988).

skill. Take time to explain to the client what the purpose of the skill is, what situations he or she might use it in, and how it will help in the long term (reduce risk).

Be sure to emphasize self-efficacy to promote the client's belief that he is capable of learning and performing the new skill and that performance of that skill will have impact on life events.

2. Describe the steps to the skill in detail.

Each step of the skill should be described in behavioral terms. There are two reasons for this. First, the client must understand all of the skill steps and how to perform them. Second, identifiable skill steps allow the officer to physically observe the steps being completed.

3. Model or demonstrate the skill.

The next part of teaching a skill is to demonstrate the skill steps for the offender. Again think back to teaching a child how to hit a ball with a bat. You have to show the skill. In this process you should use a coping rather than a mastery model. A coping model is a non-expert who therefore presents with similar difficulties to those of the imitator of the skill. A client will likely identify with a coping model more than with a mastery model; we typically learn more quickly and are willing to try new skills when they are demonstrated by those who are similar to us.[59]

4. Have the client role-play the skill.

Learning is brought about by repeated practice and reinforcement.[60] Therefore it makes sense to have the client practice the skill over and over again with correction and reinforcement. The officer should set up opportunities for the client to role-play the skill, give corrective feedback, and

---

[59] Spiegler & Guevremont (2003); Masters et al. (1979).
[60] Hergenhahn, B.R. (1976). *An introduction to theories of learning*, 2nd edition. Englewood Cliffs, NJ: Prentice-Hall, Inc.

reinforce demonstration of the skill, as well as make simple attempts at using the skill.

5. Enhance skills through homework and graduated practice.

Homework is an important part of rehearsing a skill, individualizing a generic skill, and gaining opportunities for graduated practice. Therefore, the officer should give the client homework assignments that encourage the client to use the skill outside of the office visit in real-life situations.

Exercise 2.5. Structured Skill Building

In groups of three, take the roles of client, officer, and observer.

The *client* should report that he understands the importance of making new friendships with prosocial people, but has a hard time introducing himself in new social situations.

The *officer* should teach the client how to introduce himself to others, using the following process:

1. Make sure the offender has been motivated to learn the new skill.
2. Describe the steps to the skill in detail.
3. Model or demonstrate the skill.
4. Have the offender role-play the skill.
5. Enhance skills through homework and graduated practice.

The *observer* should pay attention to the interaction to make sure the skill steps are followed by the officer and then go through the process of providing feedback.

Observer notes & feedback:

Summary

This chapter focused on developing skills to assist in forming a working relationship with offenders under your supervision. In addition, we covered aspects of coaching through giving feedback and structured skill building. The overall goal is to provide the necessary associations so that you can assist the offender in beginning to understand his or her high-risk situations and ways to either avoid or cope with those high-risk situations. As was discussed in this chapter, the working relationship you develop with the offenders under your supervision is analogous to the foundation of a house. Without a foundation, a house will eventually crumble. On the other hand, however, a foundation by itself fails to provide shelter. We now turn to those skills that, while supporting a productive association with offenders, also work to change offender behavior.

Chapter 3

Assessment, Relapse Prevention, and Session Structure

Assessment

For the past 20 years, correctional research has underscored the importance of using risk and need assessment to drive correctional case-planning, management, and risk reduction.[61] We certainly advocate that you use a risk and need assessment as part of the supervision process, and in particular a third-generation risk assessment.[62] The results of risk and need assessment should direct whom you target (the higher-risk offender) and generally what you target (criminogenic needs). However, one of the deficiencies in risk assessment is that the process itself, and the consequent results of that process, can often fail to identify *specific* targets for change for any given offender. In such cases we recommend that officers engage offenders in behavioral analysis (also known as functional

---

[61] See:

Andrews, D.A., Bonta, J., & Hoge, R. (1990). Classification for effective rehabilitation: Rediscovering psychology. *Criminal Justice and Behavior*, 17, 19-52, for an original statement on the importance of risk assessment.

Andrews, D. A., Bonta, J., & Wormith, S. J. (2006). The recent past and near future of risk and/or need assessment. *Crime and Delinquency*, 52: 7-27, for a discussion of the research and policy on risk assessment that occurred between 1990 and 2006.

[62] for examples of third-generation risk assessments see:

Bonta, J. (1996). Risk & needs assessment and treatment. In A.T. Hartland (ed.), *Choosing correctional options that work: defining the demand and evaluating the supply*, 18-32. Thousand Oaks, CA: Sage Publications, and

Andrews and Bonta (2003).

analysis). The process of risk and need assessment followed by behavioral analysis gives officers and offenders the information they need to identify specific targets (high-risk situations, people, places, things, and thoughts). The next section of this training focuses on the application and use of behavioral analysis.

> **Exercise 3.1. Identifying Risk Factors**
>
> List the factors that you think lead to criminal behavior. How do these factors lead to criminal behavior? Are these the things we should be discussing with offenders?

Behavioral Analysis

One of the questions we found many officers asked in past EPICS training is, "How do I know what to target?" We have had many discussions about this issue and find the question still persists, even in the face of risk and need assessment results. We believe the reason is that risk and need assessments are fairly gross in their measurement of needs and may not necessarily identify specific targets to attempt to change or shore up in an offender. In addition, some important criminogenic needs are not adequately captured in a meaningful way, even on 3rd & 4th generation risk assessments (such as temperament and antisocial personality patterns). For instance, a risk and need assessment instrument might tell you that an individual has antisocial peers, but it might not tell you how the person comes to be around those peers and exactly how those peers fit into his or her offending pattern. Likewise the risk and need assessment might tell you that an offender is unemployed, but it doesn't tell you why that person is unemployed or how that unemployment fits into his or her offending behavior. For example, is the offender unemployed because he or she has no marketable skills or simply because the offender dislikes employment? Does unemployment in this case create risk of offending behavior because of financial stressors or because of too much free time? Given this issue, we have included behavioral analysis as part of this curriculum.

Behavioral analysis, similar to functional analysis, is simply a process by which the offender identifies the circumstances of his or her offending behavior for the last 10 times he or she was in trouble or could have been in trouble if caught.[63] See Figure 2.1 below for a sample behavioral analysis and also the Appendix for a reproducible copy.

Completing the exercise will assist the officer in understanding the offender's past and current offending behavior, and help the offender gain understanding of his offending behavior patterns, triggers, and consequences.

Ultimately, the purpose of the behavioral analysis is to allow the officer and the offender to identify high-risk people, places, things, and thoughts (situations) that increase the offender's risk of getting into trouble. These high-risk people, places, and things should then become the focus of your interactions. You should try to get the offender to avoid these high-risk people, places, and things; if this is not possible, the offender should be taught to cope with the high-risk people, places, and things. Ultimately, over the course of supervision, the offender should be taught the skills needed to either a) avoid the situation or b) cope with the situation. In this process of the behavioral analysis, the offender and officer begin to recognize high-risk situations, discuss avoiding them, and further discuss what skill would help the offender cope with them if avoidance is not possible or fail as a strategy.[64]

Research has identified the top eight criminogenic needs associated with an increased risk of re-offending. These are: anti-social/pro-criminal attitudes, values and beliefs; pro-criminal associates and isolation from anti-criminal others; anti-social personality patterns; history of anti-social behavior; familial factors that include criminality and other psychological problems in the family of origin; low levels of personal, educational or

---

[63] For additional details on the types and examples of functional analysis, see any introductory text on behavioral therapy, such as those listed in the references of this document or Marlatt, G.A. (1985b). Situational Determinants of relapse and skill-training interventions. In G.A. Marlatt & J.R. Gordon (Eds.), *Relapse prevention*: 71-127. New York, NY: Guilford Press.

[64] These three steps form the basis of the relapse prevention component we will be talking about later (RACE).

financial achievement; lack of involvement in pro-social activities; and substance abuse. The first four are considered the big four predictors (Andrews and Bonta, 2003).[65] These should be considered top-tier needs and should be the primary focus of our interventions if they are present. The second set of needs are still related to criminal behavior; however, they are not as potent as the top tier. Some have considered these to be acute needs.[66] All of the aforementioned needs are relevant; however, if needs from the top tier are present, they should be the primary targets of services and supervision.

After a thorough review of the behavioral analysis, target the highest-risk influence from the top tier. This should not prohibit the officer from making referrals or addressing any other identified need, but the focus of the cognitive behavioral intervention must be on the highest risk need. Consider a medical example:

A recent study on the risk factors associated with heart attack, called the Inter-Heart Study, revealed that the risk factors for heart attack, in order, are: high bad-to-good cholesterol ratios, smoking, diabetes, hypertension, abdominal obesity, stress and anxiety, failure to exercise daily, failure to eat fruits and vegetables daily, and failure to consume alcohol.[67] If you went to the doctor with all nine of these risk factors and she sent you home with the instructions "consume a few glasses of wine each night" and you subsequently had a heart attack, that doctor would find herself in a malpractice lawsuit. Why? The lawsuit is likely because she failed to provide the best intervention available according to the evidence. The same applies to the field of corrections. We have a large amount of research that indicates that maladaptive cognitions, deficiencies in coping skills, and peer associations are the factors most strongly associated with criminality AND that

---

[65] Andrews & Bonta (2003).

[66] Serin, R., Mailloux, D., & Wilson, N. (2008). *Practice manual for use with the Dynamic Risk Assessment for Offender Reentry (DRAOR)*. Ottawa, ON: Carleton University.

[67] Yusuf, S., Hawken, S., Ounpuu, S., Dans, T., Avezum, A., Lanas, F., McQueen, M., Budaj, A., Pais, P., Varigos, J., Lisheng, L., on behalf of the INTERHEART Study Investigators. (2004). Effect of potentially modifiable risk factors associated with myocardial infarction in 52 countries (the INTERHEART study): case-control study. *Lancet* (364): 937-952.

targeting these needs demonstrates a consistent and appreciable reduction in recidivism relative to the targeting of the other needs mentioned above.[68] Therefore, we have to be sure to target these needs when they are present.

We recommend that the behavioral analysis be done as soon as possible after supervision starts. Because it identifies the "key" areas for any given individual, the behavioral analysis helps you identify high-risk situations the offender should avoid. Finally, the behavioral analysis helps the officer identify potential areas to monitor, behaviors to reinforce, and behaviors for which you may need to express disapproval.

Exercise 3.2. Behavioral Analysis

Looking at Figure 3.1 on the next page, what high-risk people, places, and things do you recognize for the offender? Circle high-risk places, high-risk people, and high-risk thoughts. What do you think the offender that completed this behavioral analysis needs to work on?

---

[68] See Chapter 1 for a review of some of this literature, but also see Andrews & Bonta (2003).

Figure 3.1. Sample Behavioral Analysis.

Think of the last 10 times you were in trouble. Please list the details of those circumstances below. When you return to meet with your officer, you will review this worksheet to see if there are any patterns in your life that are leading you to "high-risk" situations for getting into trouble.

When (day of week and time)	Who were you with (before/during)?	Where were you?	What were you thinking/feeling (before/during)?	What did you do?	What were you thinking/feeling after?
Monday afternoon	My dealer	With dealer at his spot	I don't want to go through withdrawal	Got high	My body felt better but I felt guilty
Tuesday afternoon	Dealer	At friend's house	I need to get high	Bought drugs and got high	I feel like crap!
Wednesday afternoon	Friend and dealer	At friend's house	Needed to get money to get high	Went hookin' to make some money	Felt terrible but looking for a high

Behavioral Analysis Interview guide

After you have collected the behavioral analysis from the offender, look for behavioral patterns. Circle anything that appears two or more times on the worksheet. Discuss each event with the offender, using the follow-up questions listed below. These questions will help you and the offender identify patterns to his or her high-risk situations.

<u>Who was with you?</u>

    Do these people typically "talk" you into engaging in criminal behavior?

    Does being around them influence you to think about committing a crime?

    Do they frequently engage in criminal behavior themselves?

    Were you in conflict with the person or persons before the behavior?

    Do they "reward" you for engaging in crime (acceptance, verbal praise, money)?

    Do they "punish" you for responsible behavior (making fun of you, not wanting to be around you)?

<u>Where were you?</u>

    Have you gotten into trouble in that place (or one similar to it) before?

    Are there often people there that get into trouble with you?

    Does illegal activity take place there?

    Is this a place that presents opportunities for you to engage in crime?

    Is this a place that triggers thoughts or feelings that are high-risk for you?

<u>What was the initiating event?</u>

    What one thing happened that led you to say to yourself, "I'm doing it" (point of no return/tipping point)?

    What were you telling yourself that made the behavior okay?

Things:

>What things were present when you got into trouble?
>
>Have these things been present before when you got into trouble?

Physical signs:

>Just before you decided to engage in the behavior, how did you feel physically (heart racing, sweaty, fidgety)?

Emotional signs:

>Just before you decided to engage in the behavior, how did you feel emotionally (angry, excited, nervous)?

Now that you have had some experience in reviewing a completed behavioral analysis, please go on to complete exercise 3.3. Before completing Exercise 3.3 be sure to review the *steps to completing the behavioral analysis* listed below:

1. Explain the document to the offender.

Tell the offender why the document is being completed. You are hoping to gain an understanding of how and why the offender ends up in situations that lead to potential legal troubles. You are also hoping that, in completing the document, the offender will be able to see some problem areas to work on.

2. Have the offender complete the document.

Tell the offender to fill out the document completely, adding as much detail as possible. You also want the offender to think about the precipitating event in the process. Sometimes a single suggestion or event sets in motion a chain of events that leads to trouble.

3. Review the completed document.

Take time to review the document looking for trends. Again be sure to focus on people, places, things, thoughts, and situations that occur two or more times.

4. Interview the offender.

Get some additional details from the offender about what has been completed. This line of questioning should involve the areas listed above: who were you with, what was the initiating event for the risky behavior, what were your thoughts and emotions, etc.

5. Ask the offender what trends he or she sees and whether the results help identify anything he or she would like to work on.

Give the offender the opportunity to review what he or she has written to identify any patterns in when she engages in risky behavior.

6. Begin developing, with the offender, targets to change in an effort to reduce risk.

Using a collaborative process, begin to identify targets to change in order to reduce the offender's risk. It is a good idea to allow the offender to comment on what you have identified; also be sure to incorporate what the offender has identified. Try to focus on major risk factors rather than minor ones.

Exercise 3.3. Behavioral Analysis Role-Play

In groups of three, take the roles of client, officer, and observer. The *client* should answer questions consistent with the behavioral analysis contained in Figure 3.2.

The *officer* should review the behavioral analysis on the Role-Play Behavioral Analysis Document and then ask the offender questions from the BA interview guide. Be sure to approach this from the standpoint of determining the offender's high-risk situations.

1. Circle anything that appears two or more times on the worksheet.
2. Discuss each event with the offender, using the follow-up questions below.

<u>Who was with you?</u>
<u>Where were you?</u>
<u>What was the initiating event?</u>
<u>What things were part of this situation?</u>

Figure 3.2. Behavioral Analysis Worksheet

Think of the last ten times you either got in trouble or got arrested. Please list out the details of those circumstances below. When you return to meet with your officer you will review this worksheet to see if there are any patterns in your life that are leading to you to "high-risk" situations for getting into trouble.

When (day of week and time)	Who were you with (before/during)?	Where were you?	What were you thinking/feeling immediately before the behavior? (Give at least 3 thoughts and 1 feeling)	What did you do? (START HERE) →	What were you thinking/feeling after? (Give at least 3 thoughts and 1 feeling)
Thursday morning	Emily	Downtown Cleveland	This is the last time I have to see my PO for 30 days. I'll be "clean" by the next visit. Emily had a really bad day and this will help her relax. Excited	Got high directly after the UDS	I fooled the system Who cares-its my life No one will know Happy, followed by extreme guilt
??? evening	Before-myself During-friends-(John and Frank)	Eastside of Cleveland	I want the pain to stop I need to stop these withdrawals John and Frank will help me, they always know where to get dope Awful, hurting	Stole a very good friend's car and purse to drive 3.5 hours north to get high	I hate myself I just betrayed one of the few people who wanted me to recover I'm worthless Depressed

When (day of week and time)	Who were you with (before/during)?	Where were you?	What were you thinking/feeling immediately before the behavior? (Give at least 3 thoughts and 1 feeling)	What did you do? (START HERE) →	What were you thinking/feeling after? (Give at least 3 thoughts and 1 feeling)
Dec 9, 2009 Evening	Emily	My Condo	I feel like shit If I don't get high I'll be dope sick We can get some easy money–it'll be a quick score with no risk Excited	Broke into the maintenance building of the development and stole tools & copper wire	Can't believe how much money we made That was so easy I can't believe how much I've disgraced my family Happy at first, then regret
May 17, 09 Morning	Frank	Abandoned warehouse	It's my 25th birthday–I deserve to have fun It'll be easy stealing from the warehouse No one is using it–they won't even notice it missing I don't want to go alone–I'll get Frank to help Excited, optimistic	Snuck in through a back door and stole roughly $800 worth of copper and property	I can't believe that I got arrested I've never been arrested before How could I be so stupid humiliated
June, 09 Middle of day	Emily	Home	My boss is such a ass Can't believe he told me not to come to work until I get cleaned up I'll show him Upset	Withdrew a large sum of money from the company account, used it to buy heroin	I'm the one who's been wronged I'm just getting even

When (day of week and time)	Who were you with (before/during)?	Where were you?	What were you thinking/feeling immediately before the behavior? (Give at least 3 thoughts and 1 feeling)	What did you do? (START HERE) →	What were you thinking/feeling after? (Give at least 3 thoughts and 1 feeling)
Friday Evening	Before-myself During-Frank	Frank's house	I need to get high I know Frank will have some dope I'll just go over for a little bit and then leave edgy	Shot up	I need to stop this Mad at myself
Wednesday afternoon	Before-Emily During-myself	The Electronics store	They deserve it for ripping people off Emily is in withdrawal and I want to make her feel better She's counting on me Nervous	Tried to steal some electronics, but the security guard was watching me so I dropped it	My luck I going to eventually run out It's only a matter of time before I get caught Disappointed that I let Emily down-knew she would be mad Relieved that I didn't do it
Sometime in May or June of 09 Night	Emily	At first at my house watching a movie-scene with a guy shooting up came on	I need to get some money to get heroin This is the quickest way to do it No one even lives there In pain	Broke into a vacant house to steal copper pipes and wire.	It was a "victimless crime" The insurance company will pay for the repairs guilty

When (day of week and time)	Who were you with (before/during)?	Where were you?	What were you thinking/feeling immediately before the behavior? (Give at least 3 thoughts and 1 feeling)	What did you do? (START HERE) →	What were you thinking/feeling after? (Give at least 3 thoughts and 1 feeling)
Over an entire week Sometime in Feb. and March of 09	Emily and her father	Carnegie Bridge	I don't want to look scared in front of Emily I want Emily's dad to think I'm tough They'll be mad if I say no Nervous	Gave in and went with them to steal copper wire from underneath the bridge	We're going to get caught for sure That was so stupid I will never do that again Mad, nervous
Jan 21, 09 Evening	Emily	Bar in Cleveland	I feel inadequate I want to impress Emily I don't want her to think I'm afraid Nervous	Shot heroin to make Emily think I wasn't afraid	I can't believe I did that After my friend died from an overdose I vowed I would never try it Guilty, hypocritical

> What physical signs did you notice in yourself?
> What emotional signs did you notice in yourself?
>
> The **observer** should pay attention to the interaction to make sure the officer follows the skill steps and then go through the process of providing feedback.
>
> Observer notes & feedback:

Recognize, Avoid, Cope, Evaluate

An integral part of the EPICS-II curriculum is the concept of RACE (Recognize, Avoid, Cope, Evaluate). RACE is based on the relapse prevention literature[69] and uses the behavioral analysis as a guide to uncover high-risk people, places, and things. RACE seeks to assist the offender in knowing how to respond to those high-risk influences to avoid getting into trouble. It is important to understand from the cognitive model[70] that high-risk situations do not **cause** a person to engage in anti-social behavior. Instead these are situations that typically elicit high-risk thoughts and feelings that can lead to criminal behavior. Whatever high-risk influences the offender encounters, the RACE steps can be used to help the offender make responsible choices. We recommend that the officer use the RACE document, along with the behavioral analysis, early in the supervision process. Stated more concretely, the issues you

---

[69] See:

Marlatt, G.A. (1985a).

Marlatt, G.A. (1985b). Situational determinants of relapse and skill-training interventions. In G. A. Marlatt & J.R. Gordon (Eds.), *Relapse prevention*: 71-127. New York, NY: Guilford Press.

Marlatt, G.A. (1985c). Cognitive factors in the relapse process. In G. A. Marlatt & J.R. Gordon (Eds.), *Relapse prevention*: 128-200. New York, NY: Guilford Press.

Dowden & Andrews (2003).

[70] To be discussed in Chapter 5.

circle on the behavioral analysis as being problematic should emerge as high-risk situations on the RACE document.

The concepts of RACE are defined below:

1. <u>R</u>ecognize high-risk influences that tempt the offender to engage in criminal behavior. These can be situations, such as people, places or things, or inaccurate perceptions, high-risk thoughts or feelings, and high-risk behaviors. An offender's first opportunity to choose responsible behavior rests in his or her ability to recognize his or her high-risk situations.

2. <u>A</u>void high-risk influences whenever possible by taking steps to stay away from situations that typically lead the offender into irresponsible choices. The best way to prevent high-risk influences from leading to irresponsible behavior is to avoid the situations in the first place. Some planning and skill development (e.g., refusal skills to be used with pro-criminal peers) might be needed before the offender can avoid high-risk situations.

3. <u>C</u>ope with high-risk influences responsibly. In situations where the high-risk influencer cannot be avoided, problem-solving techniques and other skills aid the offender in handling the situation responsibly.

4. <u>E</u>valuate your progress after each encounter in which Recognize, Avoid, and Cope were used to determine if the skills produced responsible choices and responses to high-risk situations. The offender should praise him or herself for good choices that led to positive outcomes. If the offender is not satisfied with the outcomes, he or she should either refine the skills used or change strategies so that more adaptive outcomes will occur in the future.

Implementing the steps of the RACE model will be an ongoing process throughout supervision and after the offender has been released. Follow the steps of the RACE model for each high-risk influence that affects the offender. Start with the highest-risk influence or the one that presents the biggest challenge for the offender. Take your time working through each influence and discussing strategies for each step. The steps to processing the

RACE document with a client are presented as *skill steps* on the following two pages.

1. Recognize—Identify one high-risk person, place, or thing.

This process should be related to the behavioral analysis. You might direct the offender toward selecting the most problematic or riskiest situation.

2. Develop an action plan to avoid the high-risk influence.

Can the offender reasonably avoid this high-risk influence? If YES, make sure the offender has the skills needed to avoid the high-risk influence; if NO, skip to step 3. Use the steps from problem solving to work through the action plan to avoid the high-risk situations. Remember, avoidance is NOT a passive process. It is very proactive.

For many of the personality items it will be difficult to create avoidance plans. For example, can your client avoid being impulsive in general? Probably not. If possible try to identify high-risk emotions or situations that typically trigger the impulsive response and work avoidance plans around those. For these clients it will be especially important to create well-thought-out coping plans and practice the skills needed to carry out the plans.

3. Develop an action plan for coping with the high-risk influence.

Similar to the problem-solving steps followed in #2 above, create an action plan to manage if the offender is in a situation involving the high-risk influence or if the influence CANNOT be avoided (e.g., the setting is the workplace or the influence is a family member).

Repeat the 6 steps of problem-solving (see Chapter 5 and Appendix) using the problem-solving worksheet. It is important that the offender complete the problem-solving steps for coping with the high-risk influence even if he or she has completed the steps for avoiding it. The offender must also have a contingency plan if the avoidance plan fails.

4. Evaluate the outcome.

Encourage the offender to praise or reward himself or herself immediately for attempting a new behavior (whether avoidance, new coping skills, or new thoughts) or successfully implementing the plan and avoiding irresponsible behavior. If avoidance or the coping skills did not seem to reduce risk, figure out if the skills need to be refined or new approaches need to be put into place.

Exercise 3.4. RACE Role-Play

In groups of three, take the roles of offender, officer, and observer. The *offender* should continue to answer questions and make statements based on the information presented in Figure 3.3 (the behavioral analysis).

The *officer* should complete one row of the RACE worksheet based on the information provided in the behavioral analysis and by the offender.

1. Recognize—Identify one high-risk person, place, or thing.
2. Develop an action plan to avoid the high-risk influence.
3. Develop an action plan for coping with the high-risk influence.
4. Evaluate the outcome.

The *observer* should pay attention to the interaction to make sure the officer follows the skill steps and then go through the process of providing feedback.

Observer notes & feedback:

Figure 3.3. Recognize, Avoid, Cope, Evaluate

This form is designed to help you keep track of situations (people, places, things) that increase your risk of getting into trouble. List the situations that you have recognized as being high-risk for you and how you plan to avoid them. If you can't avoid them, describe how you will cope with them. Finally, describe how your avoidance and coping strategies have worked if you have tried them out. Think of ways you can improve your avoidance and coping skills each time you try one. Last, be sure to use self-reinforcement when you avoid or cope successfully!

Recognize	Avoid Can you avoid? Plan to avoid	Cope If you cannot avoid, plan to manage	Evaluate If Used How can you better handle the scenario? What did you do well?

Structure of an Interaction

One of the important things to recognize is that supervision based on EPICS II skills requires some intentional design. That is, each interaction you have with an offender should focus on addressing target behaviors identified through the assessment and behavioral analysis process. As such, each time you have an interaction with an offender, you should ask the following questions prior to the interaction:

1. What is the purpose or goal of my interaction?
2. What should I target with this offender?
3. What are some behaviors I should look to reinforce?
4. What are some potential behaviors I might need to disapprove of?
5. What are the offender's high-risk situations?
6. What skills have we been working on?
7. What was the offender asked to do in terms of homework the last time he or she was here?

Check-in, Homework, Assess & Apply, Reinforce, Teach

To assist in covering all the bases, we have developed the CHART framework. CHART stands for:

1. Check-in: The purpose of the check-in is to determine if there are any crisis situations that need to be addressed. The offender may need to discuss these and they might need to be dealt with before being able to move on.

2. Homework: During this section of the interaction, the officer should review with the offender any homework that was assigned. This process should focus on whether the homework was completed and a review of that homework.

3. Assess & Apply: During this part of the interaction, the officer should assess how the offender applied the skill in the homework scenario or in real life. The officer should also help the offender think of additional homework scenarios or office role-plays to practice the skill. The officer should also help the offender identify foreseeable real-life situations in which the offender can use the skill.

4. Reinforce—The officer should be sure to reinforce any progress the offender has made. Completing homework assignments, attempting new skills, using mastered skills in new or more difficult or threatening situations should all be reinforced.

5. Teach—This is the process where corrective feedback and/or structured learning takes place.

Summary

This chapter introduced the behavioral assessment process, relapse prevention, and the structure of your interactions with offenders. This chapter provided both a macro and micro perspective on what supervision should look like. Both behavioral assessment at the beginning of supervision and the RACE document used throughout supervision until mastery is achieved at the end of supervision convey the macro or big picture of supervision. The structure of the interactions (CHART), on the other hand, gives you a micro picture of what individual supervision interactions should look like. Prior to meeting with each client you should walk through the different steps of CHART and have a plan for what to do at each step before interacting with the client.

Chapter 4
Bridging Skills

This chapter is called "Bridging Skills" because these skills serve as the bridge between relationship and behavioral change. As previously mentioned, a relationship is necessary but not sufficient to bring about change in an offender. Therefore, there must be a conscious shift towards changing behavior once that relationship is in place. The skills in this chapter can be thought of as bridges in the sense that they both develop and maintain a relationship and are also the basis for behavioral change. This chapter begins with a brief explanation of the model that describes the process individuals progress through when changing behavior. In this chapter we will cover three skills—reinforcement, disapproval, and effective use of authority. Conveniently, two of these skills relate to behavioral change (reinforcement and disapproval/punishment); the third, effective use of authority, gently nudges the involuntary client to do the right thing while honoring the client's right to choose and control his or her behavior.

Stages of Change

The dominant model to explain and understand behavioral change is the transtheoretical model of behavior change or the stages of change model.[71] The model emphasizes that behavioral change is a process that involves movement through a series of stages. There are five stages included: pre-contemplation (unaware),

---

[71] See Prochaska, J. O., & DiClemente, C. C. (1983). Stages and processes of self-change of smoking: Toward an integrative model of change. Journal of Consulting and Clinical Psychology, 51, 390-395.

contemplation (considering), preparation (ready and planning), action, and maintenance. While an in-depth discussion of the differences of each the stages is beyond the scope of this workbook, a brief description is included to highlight the importance of understanding that behavioral change is not a onetime event, but rather a process that occurs over time and is dependent upon internal and external contingencies.

It is not uncommon to witness frustration in an officer when confronted with a reemergence of a behavior that the officer assumed had been resolved. Movement through each of the stages can occur in either direction and individuals will frequently vacillate between stages. Clients will likely experience "slips" or relapses before achieving success.

Another important consideration is that not every client will be in the right place to make a change. Understanding the "readiness" for change of your clients will enhance your efforts in selecting appropriate interventions. For example, creating detailed action plans to avoid a high-risk influence will be less effective if the client is still in the pre-contemplation stage. Prochaska and colleagues argue that attempts to promote behavioral change are more effective if they are "stage-matched."[72]

This stage-matched model requires a brief interview exploring the client's interest in changing, which can provide considerable insight into their current stage and motivation to change. The following chart highlights some key behavioral indicators and suggested change processes of each stage. For the same client mentioned in the above example the role of the officer should initially be to help progress the client from pre-contemplation to contemplation by helping her recognize the problem behavior and increase the "pros" associated with the new behavior.

Cost-benefit analysis, a useful tool to assist in this process, is shown below. A cost-benefit analysis worksheet allows the client to explore the competing motivations associated with changing problem behaviors. The worksheet allows the client to articulate

---

[72] Prochaska, J.O. & Velicer, W.F. (1997). The transtheoretical model of health behavior change. *American Journal of Health Promotion*, 12(1): 38-48.

and examine the pros and cons of both continuing and stopping the antisocial behavior.

The cost-benefit worksheet, as displayed in Figure 4.1, has four quadrants. Quadrant I asks the client to list all the benefits of continuing the identified behavior. If the identified behavior is drug use, the benefits identified by the client might be that it helps the client relax and makes him more like his circle of friends. Quadrant II focuses on the benefits of stopping the behavior. Using the same drug use example, the benefits of stopping identified by the client might be an improved relationship with a significant other, better performance at work, and more time for family. Quadrant III shifts the discussion to cost by asking the client to identify the cost of continuing the behavior. In this case, the cost of using drugs identified by the client might be a loss of family, a loss of employment, loss of respect and an inability to be a good parent. Quadrant IV ends the discussion with a focus on the cost of stopping the behavior. If drug use is the behavior, the client might identify a loss of friends and/or an inability to deal with stress as the cost of not using. Clients should be encouraged to consider both the immediate and long-term cost and benefits.

The tug-of-war (the nature of the struggle with change) between costs and benefits of doing something different can provide insight into the client's decisional matrix. Unfortunately, the contents of the matrix don't simply come together like a simple addition problem. Instead, decisions are made based on the value given to individual elements and an understanding of how elements are connected. As clients move through the change process, the value assigned to elements is likely to shift and the recognition of how the items connect will change .[73]

---

[73] Miller & Rollnick (1991); Miller (1983)

Figure 4.1. Cost-benefit analysis

Benefits of continuing the behavior	Benefits of stopping the behavior
Cost of continuing the behavior	Cost of stopping the behavior

It is simply not possible to do justice to the comprehensive body of literature on the stages of change model and its usage in this book.[74] As we work through the bridging skills in this

---

[74] For more advanced training and understanding in motivating clients through behavioral change stages, see Grimley, Diane, Prochaska, James, Velicer, Wayne, Blais, Linelle & DiClemente, Carlo. (1994). The transtheoretical model of change. In Thomas M. Brinthaup & Richard Lipka (ed.) *Changing the self: Philosophies, techniques and experiences*: 201-226. State University of New York Press.

Cabonari, J. & DiClemente, Carlo. (2000) "Using transtheoretical model profiles to differentiate levels of alcohol abstinence." *Journal of Counseling and Clinical Psychology*, 68(5): 810-817.

Prochaska, J.O., Redding, C. & Evers, K. (2008). The transtheoretical model and stages of change. In Karen Gland, Barbara Rimer & K. Viswanath (Eds.), *Health education: Theory, research, and practice* 4th edition: 97-121. San Francisco, CA: Jossey-Bass A Wiley Imprint.

workbook, note the consistency between the goal of the bridging skills and the goals of motivational enhancement therapy.

Effective Reinforcement

Reinforcement is perhaps the most effective way to teach and elicit a new behavior. There are two ways to reinforce a behavior. After someone demonstrates the behavior you want to see repeated, you can introduce something that is pleasing to an individual (positive reinforcement) or you can take something away that is displeasing (negative reinforcement). Either way the goal of reinforcement is to strengthen the desired behavior and increase the likelihood that it will occur again in the future.[75]

The Dog Whisperer, Cesar Milan, states that it is easiest to think of reinforcement in mathematical terms. In using this example, we are in no way comparing offenders to dogs. We use Milan's description because it is so clear and concise. (As a note, however, recall from your psychology 101 classes where operant conditioning came from and how it was rigorously tested by Skinner.[76] Negative reinforcement (think mathematical symbol -) means we take something away to make it more likely that a person behaves a certain way in the future. Positive reinforcement (think mathematical symbol +) means we are adding something to make it more likely that the behavior we reinforce occurs again in the future.[77] In Milan's words, "With operant conditioning, there is positive and negative punishment and positive and negative reinforcement. Punishment reduces behaviors and reinforcement increases them. Note that the terms "positive" and "negative" are only about adding or subtracting. They have nothing to do with something being nice or not nice."

When reinforcing a behavior, we have to administer the reinforcer during or immediately following the behavior. The

---

[75] Skinner, B.F. (1953). *Science and human behavior*. New York: Macmillan.

[76] Skinner, B. F. (1963). *Operant behavior*. American Psychologist, 18: 503-515.

[77] Milan, C. & Peltier, M.J. (2010). Cesar's r*ules: Your way to train a well behaved dog*. New York, NY: Crown Publishing.

reinforcement must be contingent upon the demonstration of the behavior. The offender should be aware of getting the reinforcement due to a specific action he or she took and which specific action it is that earned the reinforcement. Reinforcement should be administered consistently and continuously when building a behavior or when it first starts to appear. As the behavior becomes part of the offender's behavioral repertoire, reinforcement might become intermittent.[78] (There are many things we can use to reinforce behavior. For example, tokens, certificates, and food would all be examples of tangible reinforcers. We can also reinforce through the introduction of privileges or activities like TV time, a field trip out of a correctional facility, or listening to music. Finally, social reinforcers are an effective option. Social reinforcers are likely the most potent, because they are natural reinforcers, there is a limitless supply of them, there is no cost associated with them, and we can administer social reinforcers almost immediately after the behavior we want to reinforce.[79]

While we support the use of tangible reinforcers and reinforcing activities, we really want to focus on effective social reinforcement, given the characteristics of social reinforcement listed above.

The steps of reinforcement are as follows[80]:

---

[78] Kazdin, A.E. (2001). *Behavior Modification in Applied Settings* (6th ed.). Belmont, CA: Wadsworth.

Kazdin, A.E. (2005). *Parent management training: Treatment for oppositional, aggressive, and antisocial behavior in children and adolescents.* New York, NY: Oxford University Press.

Spiegler & Guevremont (2003).

Baldwin, J.D., & Baldwin, J.I. (2001). *Behavior principles in everyday life*, 4th edition. Upper Saddle River, NJ: Prentice Hall; or any introductory textbook on behavioral therapy.

[79] Spiegler & Guevremont (2003).

[80] See Andrews, D.A., & Carvell, C. (1998). *Core correctional treatment — Core correctional supervision and counseling: Theory, research, assessment and practice.* Ottawa, ON: Carleton University.

Andrews & Dowden (2004).

Andrews & Bonta (2003).

Gendreau & Andrews (2002).

1. Tell the offender what she did that you like and why it is important.

Be sure to be specific, direct, and provide support that is greater than the background support you typically provide.

2. Ask the offender, in her own words and thoughts, what are the short- and long-term benefits of continuing to use the behavior you are discussing.

This step is crucial for several reasons. First, it gets the offender to articulate why the behavior is beneficial to her, which promotes cognitive change. Second, it rehearses positive thoughts associated with prosocial behavior. With ongoing rehearsal, retrieval of these thoughts comes more easily and more "automatically" when the offender is in a situation where a choice between prosocial and antisocial behavior has to be made. Third, it allows the offender to begin the process of reinforcing herself. In this way reinforcement not only increases the likelihood of a behavior occurring again in the future but also increases the efficiency of the behavior.

3. Contract with the offender to use the skill/behavior you are discussing in the future again.

This step is important too. Gaining the offender's intention to engage in a specific behavior is consistent with the research on behavioral change, which indicates that behavioral intentions are associated with actual change.[81] Just ask any salesperson. Getting a customer to agree to buy is almost as good as getting them to buy.

---

[81] Fishbein, M. (1995). Developing effective behavior change interventions: Some lessons learned from behavioral research. In T.E. Backer, S.L David & G. Soucy (Eds.) *Reviewing the behavioral sciences knowledge base on technology transfer*: 246-261. Rockville, MD: National Institute on Drug Abuse.

Exercise 4.1. Effective use of reinforcement

In groups of three, take the roles of client, officer, and observer.
The *client* should report to the office and indicate that he was at his aunt's house for Thanksgiving. He fell asleep after dinner and woke up a few minutes later to find some of his cousins smoking pot. He immediately went outside and when his aunt followed him out, he told her he couldn't be around that stuff anymore and that he had to go.

The *officer* should:
1. Tell the offender what they did that you like and why it is important.
2. Ask the offender to describe the short- and long-term benefits of continuing to use the behavior you are discussing.
3. Contract with the offender to use the skill/behavior you are discussing in the future again.

The *observer* should pay attention to the interaction to make sure the skill steps are followed by the officer and then go through the process of providing feedback.

Observer notes & feedback:

One question that repeatedly arises during coaching sessions with newly trained officers is "Am I supposed to go through all of these steps every time the client demonstrates any pro-social behavior?" The answer is *certainly not*! The use of Effective Reinforcement is not meant to replace your everyday use of verbal praise. Recognizing appropriate opportunities will enhance the effectiveness of the skill in changing offender behavior. Remember the purpose of the skill is to create cognitive change. If the client already possesses the behavior on a fairly consistent basis, it is advisable to acknowledge it, so the behavior will continue, with a few words of verbal praise, such as "great job" or "thank you," but the client is not in need of creating a new behavior. For prosocial behaviors that the client has not used in the past or has struggled to use in situations that could lead to trouble, it is important to talk through the steps of effective reinforcement. Pay close attention to any behavior that has been identified on the RACE document. Any sign of attempts to use or actual usage of these behaviors must not be ignored. Similar to techniques used in MI for evoking change talk, effective reinforcement requires selectively eliciting and responding to demonstrations of behaviors that will help the client reach his goals.

What if there is nothing to reinforce? It is not uncommon for those trained in effective reinforcement to say, "We deal with antisocial offenders, there isn't much to reinforce." This statement, in some instances, might be true. There are two ways to deal with this issue. First, an officer can begin reinforcing what are called "low-level" behaviors. For instance, if an offender needs to obtain and maintain employment but has never held a job before, it might not be too effective to wait for him to get the job before you reinforce him, as he might not get a job for months! So what should you do? If you think about the process of getting a job, when someone has never had a job before, there are a number of points where you can reinforce progress towards that goal. For example, first the client's attitudes towards legitimate (legal) work might have changed. If so, you can reinforce that change. Next, the client might make steps towards getting a job, such as completing a resume, engaging in mock interviews, and the like. These activities could also be reinforced. Finally, the client will eventually have to start looking for a job. This activity is another opportunity to reinforce. In our example the "low-level" behaviors are precursors to getting a job, the ultimate goal, but are still steps in the right direction and should therefore be reinforced.

Role-playing the skills you want to see the offender use is a second option recommended if the client isn't demonstrating any behaviors to reinforce. For example, if the offender has difficulty walking away from a conflict, you might have the offender role-play that skill with you in your office. You should then reinforce the offender's demonstration of the skill using the steps of effective reinforcement. The goal, of course, will be to get the offender to generalize the use of the skill to their real life;

however, the office environment may be a good opportunity to begin cultivating prosocial behavior and "constructing" opportunities for reinforcement.

Effective Disapproval

While reinforcement and punishment are related in some ways, they are also very distinct. However, despite differences, the techniques can be used in concert to extinguish maladaptive (antisocial) behaviors and then build new and adaptive (prosocial) replacement behaviors. Punishment is, unfortunately, limited in its ability to bring about behavioral change. We can use punishment to extinguish a behavior, but it is difficult if not impossible to punish someone into using a new behavior--especially if they don't know how to engage in that behavior[82]

There are some additional concerns when using punishment. First, those that have been exposed to punishment repeatedly can become resistant to it.[83]. Second, it can create emotional reactions that can hamper one's ability to bring about change in the recipient of the punishment. For example, some individuals who are punished experience anger or anxiety towards the person administering the punishment. Some individuals withdraw from contact completely. The primary concern is that repeated punishments can harm a relationship that must remain intact to facilitate change.[84] Finally, and we can't stress this enough, if you simply punish you will end up with what is called a behavioral gap. Punishment extinguishes behavior, but without direction and the development of an adaptive behavior to take the place of what was extinguished (through punishment), most

---

[82] Kazdin (2005).

Kazdin (2008). *The Kazdin method for parenting the defiant child.* New York, NY: Houghton Mifflin Company.

Spiegler & Guevremont (2003).

Masters et al. (1987).

[83] Kazdin (2001); Kazdin (2005).

[84] For a summary of the negative side effects of punishment, see Kazdin (2005) and Andrews & Bonta (2003).

offenders will fill the behavioral gap with another, albeit different, antisocial response.

Notwithstanding this, a good reinforcement-based program with effective punishment strategies is more effective than a good reinforcement program without punishment strategies.[85] Given the population that you serve, it is important to have some form of corrective strategy available to you.

Similar to reinforcement, we can punish by introducing something a person doesn't like or by taking away something they do like.[86] The removal of something pleasing is a type of punishment called response costs and is a very common form of punishment.[87]

While we recognize that as an officer you might have to administer punishers, we urge you to do so judiciously.[88] and be sure that you never present a corrective (role-plays, rehearsal, homework, thinking-reports) or therapeutic strategy (i.e., treatment) as a punishment. Further, we recommend that you first use effective disapproval, following the skill steps below, when offenders engage in behavior that is unacceptable.[89] The steps of effective disapproval create a cognitive link between antisocial behavior and the consequences. It also raises awareness in the client of the discrepancies between the results of his behavior and reaching his ultimate goals.

---

[85] Kazdin (2008).

[86] Miltenberger, R.G. (2004). *Behavior modification principles and procedures*, 3rd edition. Belmont, CA: Thomson Wadsworth Publishing.

[87] Thibadeau, S.F. (1998). *How to use response costs*, 2nd edition. Austin, TX: Pro-Ed, Inc.

[88] See:

Spiegler & Guevremont (2003), for general application of reinforcement and punishment.

See Wodahl, E.J., Garland, B., Culhane, S.E., & McCarty, W.P. (2011). Utilizing behavioral interventions to improve supervision outcomes in community-based corrections. *Criminal Justice & Behavior*, 38(4): 386-405, for research on the ratio of reinforcement to punishment in a community based correctional setting.

[89] Andrews & Bonta (2003).

Andrews & Carvell (1998).

Gendreau & Andrews (2002).

1. Identify the inappropriate behavior and tell the client, in an objective manner, that you disapprove of what was said or done.

In specific behavioral terms tell the client what she did that is inappropriate. You might give some reasons as to why, from your viewpoint, the behavior is unacceptable.

2. Ask the client to explore the short- and long-term consequences of continuing to engage in that behavior.

Have the client think through the short-term and long-term costs of continuing to engage in the behavior. What short-term problems can occur as a result of continuing the behavior? What long-term problems can occur as a result of continuing the behavior? This process helps the client start to develop negative thoughts about antisocial behavior and raises his awareness of the discrepancy between the consequences of this behavior and reaching his goals.

3. Ask the client to identify and discuss prosocial alternatives that could be used in place of the unacceptable behavior.

Our goal is to help the client identify potential adaptive responses she could use in the same situation in the future. You may have to make some suggestions for alternative behaviors; however, the client should really be the one generating alternatives in this step. Some prompting is acceptable. If the behavior is conducive to a role-play, practice the prosocial alternative.

4. Contract with the client to use the prosocial alternative in the future.

IF YOU ARE ADMINISTERING A PUNISHMENT, FOLLOW STEPS 5 & 6.

5. Tell the client what the consequence will be.

Note: Treatment and other corrective strategies like role-play or homework should not be a sanction or perceived as a sanction. Be sure the offender is clear on this issue.

"Because you chose to _____, then your consequences are _____."

6. Deliver the consequence.

The severity of the consequence should not rise above that which is needed to achieve a decrease in the target behavior. Be sure to watch for any adverse consequences of the punishment, such as anxiety, withdrawal, aggression, or an increase in the problematic behavior.[90]

Exercise 4.2. Effective use of disapproval

In groups of three, take on the roles of offender, officer, and observer.

The *client* should report to the officer that she got into an argument with her boyfriend last night and broke the window of his car (the window was half-way down and she pulled on it, which broke the window). The police came out when a neighbor called, but she did not get arrested or cited.

The *officer* should:

1. Identify the inappropriate behavior and tell the offender in an objective manner that you disapprove of what was said or done.
2. Ask the offender to explore the short- and long-term consequences of continuing to engage in that behavior.
3. Ask the offender to identify and discuss prosocial alternatives that could replace the unacceptable behavior.
4. Contract with the offender to use the prosocial alternative in future.

IF YOU ARE ADMINISTERING A PUNISHMENT, FOLLOW STEPS 5 & 6.

5. Tell the client what the consequence will be.
6. Deliver the consequence.

The *observer* should pay attention to the interaction to make sure

---

[90] Kazdin (2005).

> the officer follows the skill steps and then go through the process of providing feedback.
>
> Observer notes & feedback:

Effective Use of Authority

One of the major emphases of cognitive behavioral therapy, which is the backbone of this training, is that everything is a personal choice and that we have control over our choices.[91] This idea is also represented in other therapeutic and clinical approaches to changing behavior, such as motivational interviewing.[92] It is important when we communicate with offenders that we emphasize that everything is a personal choice and they have complete control over the choices they make. This emphasis not only gives control back to the offender but also places responsibility and accountability for decisions upon him or her. This process also reduces resistance or can diffuse resistance, as a common response to perceived or real loss of choice and control is to assert one's liberty.[93]

Nonetheless, staff in correctional settings has a position of authority over the offenders you come in contact with. There is an entire body of research on the different types of authority in correctional settings. The skill discussed in this section focuses on how to use that authority effectively. Most effective is a firm but fair approach.[94] A firm but fair approach entails monitoring for

---

[91] See for example:

Ellis, A., & Dryden, W. (1997). *The practice of rational emotive behavior therapy*. New York: Springer.

Beck, A. T. (1976). *Cognitive Therapy and Emotional Disorders*. New York: International Universities Press.

[92] Miller & Rollnick (2001).

[93] Miller & Rollnick (2001).

[94] Andrews & Bonta (2003).

Skeem et al. (2007).

compliance and encouraging offenders to make appropriate and adaptive choices, while recognizing their freedom to choose and control their behavior. This is of course in addition to monitoring for and correcting noncompliance.

The skill steps to this skill, consistent with the notions above, are listed below and are adapted from Andrews & Carvell (1998) and Gendreau and Andrews (2002)[95]:

1. Identify a situation where the offender is in a decision-making position.

This might be a decision point where the offender is heading down the wrong path, e.g., noncompliance with supervision or verbally indicating he will be noncompliant.

2. Present the available choices and the attendant consequences of each choice

This process should be objective and honest. The officer should avoid doomsday ultimatums and simply state the options for the offender and the realistic consequences for the offender following either of those choices. The officer should encourage compliance and reinforce it if that is the choice that is made. Again, be sure to stress that the choice is up to the offender; it is his or hers to make.

3. At the next available opportunity, follow up by determining if objectives were met (which choice did the offender choose?).

The officer should, at the next opportunity, follow up with the offender to see what choice was made. The officer should either reinforce or disapprove of the choice. Regardless of the choice the offender made, the consequences stipulated in step 2 should be delivered.

Paparrozzi & Gendreau (2005).
[95] Andrews & Carvell (1998); Gendreau & Andrews (2002).

4. In general, look for and reward compliance.

As a regular part of interactions, be sure to look for and reinforce compliance with rules and conditions of supervision, acquisition of new skills, and prosocial behavior in general.

Exercise 4.3. Effective use of authority

In groups of three, take the roles of offender, officer, and observer.

The *offender* should report to the officer. She has been resistant to participating in substance abuse treatment since the beginning of supervision. While she did attend an AOD assessment, she does not want to follow through with the recommended treatment (IOP). She reports to the officer that she is not going to her intake appointment the following day.

The *officer* should:

1. Identify a situation where the offender is in a decision-making position.
2. Present the available choices and the attendant consequences of each choice.
3. At the next available opportunity, follow up by determining if objectives were met (which choice did he/she choose?).
4. In general, be sure to look for and reward compliance.

The *observer* should pay attention to the interaction to make sure the skill steps are followed by the officer and then go through the process of providing feedback.

Observer notes & feedback:

> **Exercise 4.4. When to use disapproval and when to use effective authority**
>
> Take ten minutes at your table and come up with as many behaviors or instances where you would use disapproval or effective use of authority. We will discuss your answers in a large group so be sure to elect a scribe and spokesperson.

Summary

This chapter has focused on three skills that continue to develop a good working relationship with clients and maintain that relationship. The skills covered in this chapter also begin to provide some behavioral direction for the offender. Reinforcement should be used to increase the likelihood of particular behaviors. While you may not use the full set of reinforcement steps for every behavior the offender demonstrates, you do want to always reinforce prosocial behavior. For example, if an offender has a hard time showing up for appointments on the scheduled day, when he does show up on the right day, you might go through the full set of reinforcement steps. For a different offender who always shows up on time, you might reinforce that behavior by saying, "Hey, thanks for showing up on your scheduled day. I know how hard it is for you to get down here and I appreciate the effort," rather than using the full set of steps. Effective disapproval should be used any time the offender engages in antisocial or maladaptive behavior. Through repetition you want to change the offender's thoughts about that particular problem behavior and begin, almost automatically, to use the alternative adaptive behavior identified in the skill steps of disapproval. Finally, we presented the effective use of authority as an option that gives offenders control of the decision-making process while being open and honest about the consequences of their actions. This skill might seem very similar to the idea of "Emphasizing Personal Choice and Control" listed in the previous chapter. While there are great similarities between the two, effective use of authority is a bit more directive in that you are nudging the individual towards compliance.

The skills presented in this chapter certainly help you begin to shape clients' behavior and begin the process of changing how a client thinks about risky behaviors. The next chapter, Intervention Skills, provides some information that will assist you in directly targeting and changing how your clients think and behave. We also provide some basic skills (problem solving and time out) that will assist offenders in dealing with high-risk situations.

Chapter 5

Intervention Skills

Cognitive Model

Cognitive Behavioral Therapy (CBT) is a form of psychotherapy that arose in the 1950s from a merger of Cognitive and Behavioral Therapies.[96] Originally, CBT was not a technique for rehabilitating offenders, but rather a briefer, more time-limited, form of therapy aimed at treating specific psychological disorders, such as anxiety or psychotic disorders. It was not until the 1970s that Samuel Yochelson and Stanton Samenow pioneered the use of CBT within the criminal population.[97] Current research establishes CBT as an evidence-based form of treatment and shows that it yields the strongest, most consistent benefit in reducing recidivism.[98]

CBT emphasizes the important role that thoughts and feelings play in determining behavior. In essence, CBT states that our

---

[96] Spiegler & Guevremont (2003).

[97] Samenow, S. (1984). *Inside the criminal mind.* New York: Crown Publishers.

Yochelson, S. & S. Samenow. (1977). *The criminal personality*, Volume 1. Chicago: Jason Aronson.

[98] For systematic reviews see:

Lipsey, M.W., Chapman, G.L. & Landenberger, N.A. (2001). *Cognitive-behavioral programs for offenders.* The Annals of the American Academy of Political and Social Science, 578: 144-157.

Wilson, D. B., Bouffard, L. A. & Mackenzie, D. L. (2005). A quantitative review of structured, group-oriented, cognitive-behavioral programs for offenders. *Criminal Justice & Behavior*, 32: 172 – 204.

Pearson, F.S., Lipton, D.S., Cleland, C.M., & Yee, D.S. (2002). The effects of behavioral/cognitive behavioral programs on recidivism. *Crime and Delinquency*, 48: 476-496.

thoughts about a particular external situation, rather than the situation itself, determine our behavior in response to that situation. The benefit of this is that even though most situations are outside our control, we do have control over our thoughts and therefore our behavior.[99] By introducing the cognitive model (Figure 2) to the offender, the officer can begin the process of restructuring antisocial thoughts and help the offender learn to replace them with alternative, pro-social thoughts, which lead to changes in behavior. Teaching this model helps the offender see and understand the connection between thinking and behavior. The cognitive model is an easy-to-understand, pictorial representation of how events can trigger thoughts/feelings, which cause the behavior. For many offenders, behaviors happen so quickly and automatically that they pay little attention to the thoughts that come in between. By initiating a discussion about the cognitive model, officers can help offenders start the process of identifying and paying attention to high-risk thoughts that typically have led to irresponsible behavior and creating new thinking patterns likely to decrease criminal behavior.

Among key terms in explaining the cognitive model are thoughts and replacement thoughts. In this model there are external and internal events. An external event is anything that happens outside your control. External events are things like someone cutting you off in traffic, spilling coffee on you, yelling at you, etc. They are things that you cannot control. Internal events are **thoughts** that we have about the external event. **Thoughts** include attitudes, thoughts, values, and beliefs that a person experiences in response to an event. They are seemingly automatic in that they might be quickly recalled when an event occurs. These thoughts are at times so automatic that the offender might not even be aware

---

[99] Beck, A.T. (1970). Cognitive therapy: Nature and relation to behavior therapy. *Behavior Therapy*, 1: 184-200.

Beck, A.T. (1976). *Cognitive therapy and emotional disorders*. New York: International Universities Press.

Ellis, A. (1991). The revised ABC's of Rational-Emotive Therapy (RET). *Journal of Rational-Emotive and Cognitive-Behavior Therapy*, 9: 139-172.

Ellis, A. (2001). *Overcoming destructive beliefs, feelings, and behaviors*. Amherst, NY: Prometheus Books.

that they are occurring. These thoughts may provide direct support for engaging in criminal behavior (e.g., "it's okay to beat someone up if they disrespect you"), or they may provide indirect support by neutralizing or justifying the criminal behavior (e.g., "corporations have insurance to cover the loss, so my stealing didn't really hurt anyone"). **Thoughts** can occur before the behavior, thereby supporting its use, and/or after a behavior, thereby excusing or justifying its use. Once a problematic thought is identified, the process of cognitive restructuring begins by developing **replacement thoughts**. **Replacement thoughts** are alternative thoughts that replace the old thoughts to help produce new outcomes. Start by explaining the purpose and components of the *cognitive model* using the *steps* listed below.

1. Identify a problem behavior or situation that would benefit from the cognitive model and offer the model as a solution.

a. Choose a non-threatening example like being cut off in traffic or someone bumping into you.

b. Use the hand-out (Fig. 5.1) as a guide.

2. Explain the three main components of the cognitive model.

a. Explain that there are external events that occur, internal events (our thoughts), and then our behavior.

b. Stress the importance of paying attention to the internal thoughts that occur in response to the external situation that led to the behavior.

c. Explain to the offender how developing replacement thoughts can lead to different behavior.

3. Ask the offender to examine his situation using the cognitive model.

a. Discuss how initial thoughts lead to one outcome and replacement thoughts would lead to another.

4. Contract with the offender to use the cognitive model in a future situation.

a. If time permits, work through a real-life example.

b. Take notes using the hand-out Figures 5.1 and 5.2.

Exercise 5.1. Teaching the Cognitive Model

In groups of three, take the roles of offender, officer, and observer.

The *offender*, who has a problem with gambling, reports that he has a hard time driving past the casinos on his way to work. The last time he gambled he ended up in serious debt, relapsed, and had all sorts of problems in his relationship with his wife. When he reports, he says that as he drives by the casinos he feels the pull and remembers all those times he "won it big." He kept on driving this time, but doesn't know how long he can keep passing up the opportunity for some quick cash.

Using Figure 2, the *officer* should teach the cognitive model to the offender in the following steps:

1. Identify a problem behavior or situation that would benefit from the cognitive model and offer the model as a solution.
2. Explain the three main components of the cognitive model.
3. Ask the offender to examine his situation using the cognitive model.
4. Contract with the offender to use the cognitive model in a future situation.

The *observer* should pay attention to the interaction to make sure the officer follows the skill steps and then go through the process of providing feedback.

Figure 5.1. Pictorial of Cognitive Model

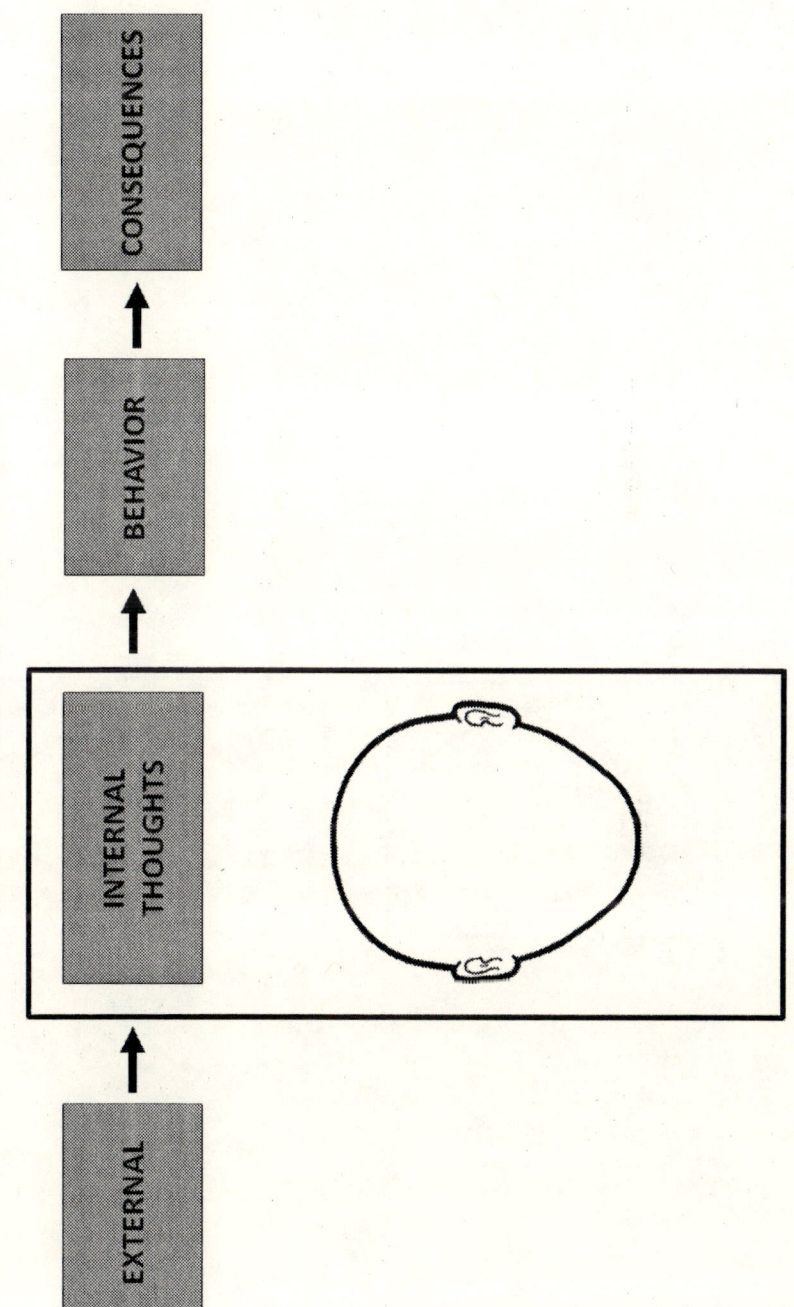

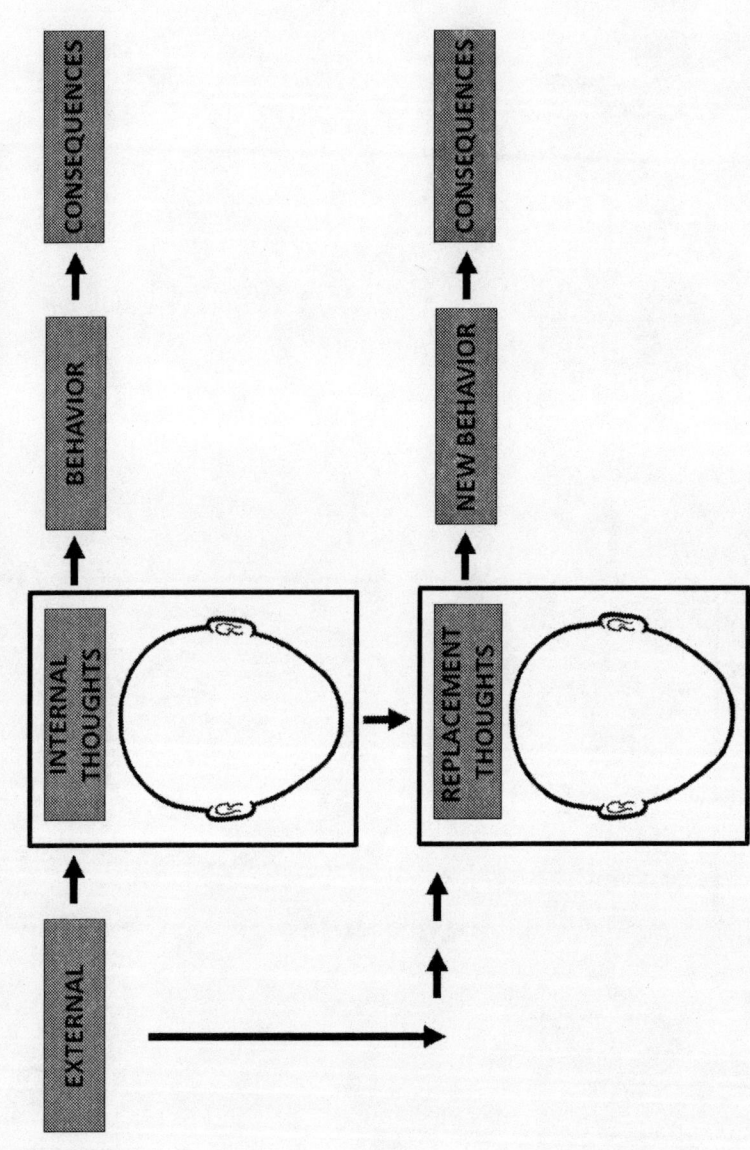

Figure 5.2. Pictorial of Cognitive Model with Replacement Thoughts

> Observer notes & feedback:

Applying and Reviewing the Cognitive Model

Throughout the course of supervision, encourage the offender to complete additional thinking reports as homework assignments. Select high-risk situations from the behavioral analysis worksheet and ask the offender to work through them to develop replacement thoughts, coping skills, and avoidance plans. The offender should also keep several blank worksheets to complete on new situations as they occur. Be prepared to discuss the homework assignments during scheduled visits. Talk through the offender's replacement thoughts and help him or her decide whether they would be effective in reducing irresponsible behavior. Be open to conducting role-plays to provide additional practice in implementing the replacement thoughts. Read through the steps for reviewing the application of the cognitive model:

1. Ask if the client completed the assignment.

Throughout the course of supervision, you should be assigning the completion of thinking reports. You should be using these in a proactive manner, based on scenarios you develop that relate to the high-risk situations identified in the behavioral analysis and other high-risk situations that occur.

2. Ask the client to describe the situation used to practice the skill.

The client should provide a description, in objective terms, of the situation that she is applying the model to. Be sure to look for links to the high-risk situations (HRS) identified in the behavioral analysis. If the client is not applying the model to HRSs, be sure to direct him or her to do so for the next homework assignment.

3. Ask the client to present the thought (old way of thinking) and replacement thoughts (new way of thinking) that occurred in the situation.

Walk through the cognitive model with the client. Let the client present all the completed material before giving any feedback. Then follow the steps for giving feedback.

4. Ask the client to describe the resulting behavior.

Determine the outcome of the application of the model. Did the client identify replacement thoughts and use them, resulting in a different behavior?

5. Reinforce and correct with feedback.

You should reinforce the client for attempting to or completing the homework. The client should be reinforced for successful or attempted use of the model. You should also reinforce new replacement behaviors. Be sure to correct any deficiencies with feedback and be prepared to role-play the corrected scenario. Remember, practice only makes perfect if you are practicing perfectly.

Exercise 5.2. Applying the Cognitive Model

In groups of three, take the roles of offender, officer, and observer.

The *offender* reports to the office and indicates that she used the model to change her decision about going out with her friends. She has completed the following worksheet and is prepared to discuss it with you.

The *officer* should walk through the application of the cognitive model with the offender:

1. Ask if the offender completed the assignment.
2. Ask the offender to describe the situation used to practice the skill.
3. Ask the offender to present the thoughts and replacement thoughts that occurred in the situation.
4. Ask the offender to describe the resulting behavior.
5. Reinforce or disapprove of the resulting behavior.

Figure 5.3. Completed Worksheet for Exercise 5.2

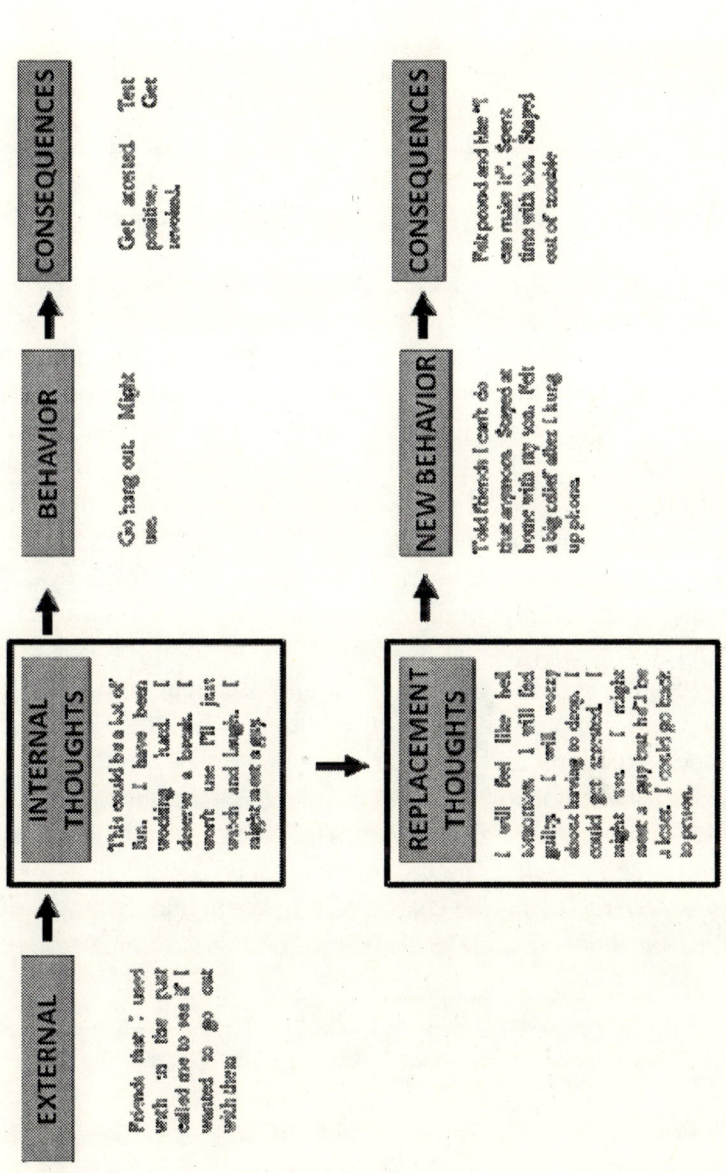

> The ***observer*** should pay attention to the interaction to make sure the officer follows the skill steps and then go through the process of providing feedback.
>
> Observer notes & feedback:

Problem-Solving Skills

A problem is defined as a situation that demands a response, although no effective response is immediately apparent or available to the person confronted with the situation, due to one or more obstacles. Simply put, a problem is a situation without a known or readily available solution.[100] Problems may also be referred to as high-risk situations. The source of a problem situation can be the environment (task-oriented demands), interpersonal conflict (conflict in the demands or expectations of two or more people), or internal obstacles, including our cognitive response to environmental factors and interpersonal conflict.[101]

Problem solving is a cognitive-behavioral process typically taught from a skill deficit model that proposes that high-risk situations are handled inappropriately because offenders lack the skills to process problem situations and respond appropriately. The process is often taught as a method of reducing involvement in antisocial behaviors and promoting prosocial behavior. The core concepts of the problem-solving process include identifying a perceived challenge, identifying options and surveying the cost/benefit of each, and making a decision on the best action to achieve the desired outcome.[102]

---

[100] D'Zurilla, T.J. & Goldfried, M.R. (1971). Problem solving and behavior modification. *Journal of Abnormal Psychology*, 78:107-126.

[101] See:

Marlatt (1985a).

Marlatt (1985b).

Marlatt (1985c).

[102] Bush, J., Glick, B., & Taymans, J. (1996). *Thinking for a change: An integrated cognitive behavior change program*. Longmont, CO: National Institute of Corrections.

Problem solving is often chosen as an intervention technique because it is a generic behavior management approach with broad applicability. Problem solving can be taught to a wide range of clients; and can be generalized to target many different types of high-risk behaviors. For example, impulsive clients who develop problem-solving skills learn to avoid the immediate response and think through problem situations. A high-risk person in the criminal justice system often lacks the ability to generate options and regularly views problems through a black and white lens. Learning problem solving demonstrates that most situations have more than one possible solution; this allows the problem solver to practice generating prosocial options.

Some problems require an immediate response, but others allow us more time to work through the problem-solving process. It is important to use the problem-solving process to deal with both types of problems, but we'll focus on the more immediate problems. This will allow us to practice using the problems that generally lead to the impulsive response that often has consequences we would like to avoid.

Based on the relevant literature (cited in footnote 102, we propose the following steps to problem solving:

1. Stop & Think and Identify the Problem

a. Help the client identify when he or she has a problem by discussing the cues that might serve as a warning sign. Warning signs include thoughts, feelings, and physical reactions (such as sweaty palms, increased heart rate, and clenched fist) that happen in response to an external event or circumstance.

b. Help the client describe the problem objectively. The description should begin with "I" and objectively detail the reason for the warning signs and your risk. Example: I have sweaty palms, because I am being confronted by my boss

---

Goldstein (1988).

Goldstein, A., & Glick, B. (1987). *Aggression replacement training: A comprehensive Intervention for aggressive youth.* Champaign, IL: Research Press.

about an assignment. This puts me at risk, because I might yell and blame her for not getting information to me on time.

2. Generate Alternative Solutions and Choose Your Best Option

a. Brainstorm with the client by developing a list of solutions that are alternatives to the risky behavior identified in step one (I might yell and blame her for not getting information to me on time) and options for achieving the goal identified in step three.

b. Simply list the possible options without judgment.

c. Once all options are identified, review EACH option and identify the short- and long-term consequences of each.

d. Choose the option that is an alternative to the risky behavior, helps achieve the identified goal, and has short-term and long-term consequences that don't lead to future problem situations.

Exercise 5.3. Problem Solving

In groups of three, take the roles of offender, officer, and observer.

The *offender* should report that she has had a hard time dealing with a co-worker at her place of employment. This person gives her a hard time about the job she does and says things to her that make her really angry. The other co-worker, even though she is a peer, tells her what to do and when to do it. She thinks the co-worker does this because the co-worker looks down on her, since she has been to prison and is on parole. The other day, after this co-worker told her that she does a terrible job, the offender walked off the job.

The *officer* should go through problem solving with the offender, making sure to cover each step below. Use the problem-solving worksheet when teaching this skill.

1. Stop and Think and Identify the Problem
2. Generate Alternative Solutions and Choose Your Best Option

The *observer* should pay attention to the interaction to make sure the officer follows the skill steps and then go through the process of providing feedback.

Observer notes & feedback:

Figure 5.4. Problem Solving Worksheet

Step 1. State the problem	
Step 2. Generate options	**Evaluate options**
Option 1.	Costs
	Benefits
Option 2.	Costs
	Benefits
Option 3.	Costs
	Benefits
Option 4.	Costs
	Benefits
ADVANCED PLANNING Choose an option—I choose option #	
The steps I'll use to accomplish my plan are: 1. 2. 3. 4. 5. 6.	

Put the plan into action (who, what, when, where)
I will use the plan in the following situations....   I will use the plan with the following people....   I will use the plan at the following times....
Evaluate the plan
What went well?   Do I do all the steps?   What was the outcome?   Do I need more practice with the plan (role play)?   Do I need a new plan?

Time-Out

Many inmates state that they have difficulty in readjusting to living at home. For many this involves acclimating to families that they haven't seen in months or even years. Family dynamics change and offenders returning home can find this new dynamic difficult to navigate. That's why it is important to ensure that offenders have skills to avoid domestic violence situations, especially if they have a history of domestic violence. Based on Gondolf's 2002 research, it appears that the simple skill of Time-Out can be used to avoid some domestic violence situations.[103] The skill steps of Time-Out are fairly straightforward and the officer should use the

---

[103] Gondolf, E. W. (2002). *Batter intervention systems*. Thousand Oaks, CA: Sage Publications.

Time-Out skill sheet in the appendix and teach the offender the skill, using structured skill building.

The process for teaching Time-Out is similar to that for other skills. Remember to use those structure skill-building steps we covered in chapter 1. Be sure to lead the offender through the Time-Out worksheet in the appendix. Role-play the skill a number of times, being sure to troubleshoot along the way and provide feedback. Contract with the offender to use the skill, give the offender the Time-Out skills worksheet, and tell him or her that you will be following up on the use of the skill.

Exercise 5.5. Time-Out

In groups of three, take the roles of client, officer, and observer.

The *client* should report that he has had domestic abuse problems in the past, was taught the skill of Time-Out in the past, but doesn't really remember it. The client reports that he has been getting into arguments with his wife recently; they got into a heated argument last night and, while he didn't touch her, she called the police. He was not arrested or cited, but they did put him in the back of the cruiser until they sorted everything out. He thinks his wife called the police because she was scared, given his history of hitting her. He spent the night at his mother's house to give things a chance to settle down.

The *officer* should teach the client Time-Out and have him role-play the Time-Out skill. You can use the Time-Out worksheet included in the Appendix.

The *observer* should pay attention to the interaction to make sure the officer follows the skill steps and then go through the process of providing feedback.

Observer notes & feedback:

Summary

This chapter has presented four skills that can be used to change the way your clients think and behave. We presented two skills related to the cognitive model and two coping skills that assist clients in developing problem-solving skills and dealing with domestic abuse. These skills need to be used repeatedly by clients so that they become "second nature" and their first response when in high-risk situations. This process is achieved through repetition, practice, and constructive feedback. We hope that the clients on your caseload will master all of these skills, when relevant, before being discharged from supervision.

This training was designed to enhance the effectiveness of our correctional interventions, including community supervision. We hope that you have found these materials useful. Much of what you see here has been suggested and refined through the comments of correctional practitioners like you. We look forward to hearing from you so that we can modify these materials to make them even more useful to officers, offenders, and communities.

References

Andrews, D.A. (1999). Assessing program elements for risk reduction: The correctional program assessment inventory. In Patricia M. Harris (Ed.). *Research to results: Effective community corrections.* (pp. 151-170). Lanham, MD: American Correctional Association.

Andrews, D. A., & Bonta, J. (2003). *The psychology of criminal conduct* (3rd ed.). Cincinnati, OH: Anderson.

Andrews, D. A., Bonta, J., & Hoge, R. (1990). Classification for effective rehabilitation: Rediscovering psychology. *Criminal Justice and Behavior*, 17, 19-52.

Andrews, D. A., Bonta, J., & Wormith, S. J. (2006). The recent past and near future of risk and/or need assessment. *Crime and Delinquency*, 52: 7-27.

Andrews, D.A. & Kiessling, J.J. (1980). Program structure and effective correctional practices. A summary of CaVIC research. (pp. 441-463). In R.R. Ross & P. Gendreau (Eds.), *Effective correctional treatment.* Toronto: Butterworths.

Andrews, D.A., Keissling, J.J., Russell, R.J. & Grant, B.A. (1979) Volunteers and the one to one supervision of adult probationers. Toronto: Ontario Ministry of Correctional Services.

Andrews, D. A., & Carvell, C. (1998). *Core correctional treatment — Core correctional supervision and counseling: Theory, research, assessment and practice.* Ottawa, ON: Carleton University.

Andrews, D.A., Zinger, I., Hoge, R., Bonta, J., Gendreau, P. & Cullen, F. (1990) Does correctional treatment work? A clinically relevant and psychologically informed meta-analysis. *Criminology* 28 (3): 369-401.

Baldwin, J.D., & Baldwin, J.I. (2001). *Behavior principles in everyday Life*, 4th edition. Upper Saddle River, NJ: Prentice Hall.

Bandura, A. (1994). Self-efficacy. In V. S. Ramachaudran (Ed.), *Encyclopedia of human behavior* (Vol. 4, pp. 71-81). New York: Academic Press. (Reprinted in H. Friedman [Ed.], *Encyclopedia of mental health*. San Diego: Academic Press, 1998).

Beck, A. T. (1970). Cognitive therapy: Nature and relation to behavior therapy. *Behavior Therapy*, 1: 184-200.

Beck, A. T. (1976). *Cognitive therapy and emotional disorders*. New York: International Universities Press.

Beck, A. T. (1991). Cognitive therapy: A 30 year retrospective. *American Psychologist*, 46: 368-375.

Bonta, J. (1996). Risk & needs assessment and treatment. In A. T. Hartland (Ed.), *Choosing correctional options that work: Defining the demand and evaluating the supply*, 18-32. Thousand Oaks, CA: Sage Publications.

Bonta, J., Bourgon, G., Rugge, T., Scott, T., Yessine, A.K., Gutierrez, L., & Li, J. (2010). *The Strategic training initiative in community supervision: Risk-need-responsivity in the real world*. Ottawa, ON: Public Safety.

Bonta, J., Rugge, T., Scott, T.-L., Bourgon, G. & Yessine, A. (2008) Exploring the black box of community supervision, *Journal of Offender Rehabilitation*, 47: 248-270.

Bonta, J., Rugge, T., Sedo, B., & Coles, R. (2004). *Case management in Manitoba probation*. Public Safety and Emergency Preparedness, Canada.

Bush, J., Glick, B., & Taymans, J. (1996). *Thinking for a change: An integrated cognitive behavior change program*. Longmont, CO: National Institute of Corrections.

Cabonari, J. & DiClemente, Carlo. (2000) Using transtheoretical model profiles to differentiate levels of alcohol abstinence. *Journal of Counseling and Clinical Psychology*, 68(5): 810-817.

California Department of Corrections. (2009). *Corrections Moving Forward*. Sacramento, CA: Office of Public and Employee Communications.

Camp, C. & G. Camp (2003). *The corrections yearbook, adult corrections 2002*. Middletown, CT: The Criminal Justice Institute, Inc.

Cullen, F. T. (2011). Taking rehabilitation seriously: Creativity, science, and the challenge of offender change. *Punishment and Society* (in press).

DeMichele, M.T. (2007). *Probation and parole's growing caseloads and workload allocation: Strategies for managerial decision making*. Lexington, KY: The American Probation & Parole Association.

Dowden, C. & Andrews, D. A. (1999a). What works for female offenders: A meta-analytic review. *Crime and Delinquency*, 45: 438-452.

Dowden, C. & Andrews, D. A. (1999b). What works in young offender treatment: A meta-analysis. *Forum on Corrections Research*, 11: 21-24.

Dowden, C. & Andrews, D.A. (2004). The importance of staff practices in delivering effective correctional treatment: A meta-analytic review of core correctional practices. *International Journal of Offender Therapy and Comparative Criminology*, 48: 203-214.

Dowden, C. Antonowicz, D., & Andrews, D.A. (2003). The effectiveness of relapse prevention with offenders: A meta-analysis. *International Journal of Offender Therapy and Comparative Criminology*, 47:516-528.

D'Zurilla, T.J. & Goldfried, M.R. (1971). Problem solving and behavior modification. *Journal of Abnormal Psychology*, 78:107-126.

Ellis, A. (1991). The revised ABC's of Rational-Emotive Therapy (RET). *Journal of Rational-Emotive and Cognitive-Behavior Therapy*, 9: 139-172.

Ellis, A. (2001). *Overcoming destructive beliefs, feelings, and behaviors*. Amherst, NY: Prometheus Books.

Ellis, A., & Dryden, W. (1997). *The practice of rational emotive behavior therapy.* New York: Springer.

Fishbein, M. (1995). Developing effective behavior change interventions: Some lessons learned from behavioral research. In T.E. Backer, S.L David & G. Soucy (Eds.) *Reviewing the behavioral sciences knowledge base on technology transfer*: 246-261. Rockville, MD: National Institute on Drug Abuse.

Gendreau, P. (1996). The principles of effective interventions with offenders. In Alan T. Harland (Ed.), *Choosing correctional options that work: Defining the demand and evaluating the supply*: 117-130. Thousand Oaks, CA: Sage.

Gendreau, P. & Andrews, D.A. (1994). *The correctional program assessment inventory.* Saint John, Canada: University of New Brunswick.

Gendreau, P. & Andrews, D. A. (2002). *The correctional program assessment inventory 2000.* (CPAI 2000). Saint John, Canada: University of New Brunswick.

Gendreau, P., Little, T., & Goggin, C. (1996). A meta-analysis of the predictors of adult offender recidivism: What works! *Criminology*, 34: 575-607.

Goldstein, A., & Glick, B. (1987). *Aggression replacement training: A comprehensive intervention for aggressive youth.* Champaign, IL: Research Press

Goldstein, A.P. (1988). *The prepare curriculum teaching prosocial competencies.* Champaign, IL: Research Press.

Gondolf, E. W. (2002). *Batter intervention systems.* Thousand Oaks, CA: Sage Publications.

Gordon, T., (1970). *Parent effectiveness training.* New York: Peter H. Wyden.

Green, D.P. & Winik, D. (2010). Using random judge assignments to estimate the effects of incarceration and probation on recidivism among drug offenders. *Criminology* 48(2): 357-386.

Grimley, Diane, Prochaska, James, Velicer, Wayne, Blais, Linelle & DiClemente, Carlo. (1994). The transtheoretical model of change. In Thomas M. Brinthaup & Richard Lipka (Ed.) *Changing the self: Philosophies, techniques and experiences*: 201-226. State University of New York Press.

Hadfield-Law, L. (2002). *Train your team yourself: How to design & deliver effective in-house training courses.* Oxford, U.K.: How To Books Ltd.

Hergenhahn, B.R. (1976). *An Introduction to Theories of Learning*, 2nd edition. Englewood Cliffs, NJ: Prentice-Hall, Inc.

Jones-Hubbard, Dana and Travis C. Pratt. (2002). A Meta-analysis of the predictors of delinquency among girls. *Journal of Offender Rehabilitation*, 34(3):1-13.

Kazdin, A.E. (2001). *Behavior modification in applied settings* (6th ed.). Belmont, CA: Wadsworth.

Kazdin, A.E. (2005). *Parent management training: Treatment for oppositional, aggressive, and antisocial behavior in children and adolescents.* New York, NY: Oxford University Press.

Kazdin, A.E. (2008). *The Kazdin Method for parenting the defiant child.* New York, NY: Houghton Mifflin Company.

Langan, P.A., and Levin, D.J. (2002). *Recidivism of prisoners released in 1994.* Washington D.C.: Bureau of Justice Statistics.

Lipsey, M.W., Chapman, G.L. & Landenberger, N.A. (2001). Cognitive-behavioral programs for offenders. *The Annals of the American Academy of Political and Social Science*, 578: 144-157.

Lopez-Viets, V., Walker, D.D., & Miller, W.R. (2002). What is motivation to change? A scientific analysis. In M. McMurran (Ed.), *Motivating offenders to change: A guide to enhancing engagement in therapy.* Chichester, UK: John Wiley & Sons Ltd.

Marlatt, G.A. (1985a). Relapse prevention: Theoretical rationale and overview of the model. In G. A. Marlatt & J.R. Gordon (Eds.), *Relapse prevention*: 3-70. New York, NY: Guilford Press.

Marlatt, G.A. (1985b). Situational determinants of relapse and skill-training interventions. In G. A. Marlatt & J.R. Gordon (Eds.), *Relapse prevention*: 71-127. New York, NY: Guilford Press.

Marlatt, G.A. (1985c). Cognitive factors in the relapse process. In G. A. Marlatt & J.R. Gordon (Eds.), *Relapse prevention*: 128-200. New York, NY: Guilford Press.

Martinson, R. (1974). What works?—Questions and answers about prison reform. *The Public Interest*, 35: 22-54.

Martinson, R., & Wilks, J. (1977). Save parole supervision. *Federal Probation* 41: 23-27.

Masters, J. C., Burish, T.G., Hollon, S.D., & Rimm, D.C. (1987). *Behavior therapy techniques & empirical findings*, 3rd edition. San Diego, CA: Harcourt Brace Jovanovich, Publishers.

Milan, C. & Peltier, M.J. (2010). *Cesar's rules: Your way to train a well behaved dog*. New York, NY: Crown Publishing.

Miller, W. R., & Rollnick, S. (2002). *Motivational interviewing: Preparing people for change*. New York: Guilford Press.

Miltenberger, R.G. (2004). *Behavior modification principles and procedures*, 3rd edition. Belmont, CA: Thomson Wadsworth Publishing.

Nesovic, A. (2003). *Psychometric evaluation of the correctional program assessment inventory (CPAI)*. Carleton University: Doctoral Dissertation.

Palmer, T. (1965). Types of treaters and types of juvenile offenders. *Youth Authority Quarterly*, 18: 14-23.

Palmer, T. (1973). Matching worker and client in corrections. *Social Work*, 18: 95-103.

Palmer, T. (1975). Martinson revisited. *Journal of Research in Crime and Delinquency*, 12: 131-152.

Palmer, T. (1991). The effectiveness of intervention: Recent trends and current issues. *Crime and Delinquency*, 37: 330-346.

Palmer, T. (1994). *A profile of correctional effectiveness and new directions for research*. Albany, NY: SUNY Press.

Palmer, T. (1995). Programmatic and nonprogrammatic aspects of successful intervention: New directions for research. *Crime and Delinquency*, 41: 100-131.

Panyan, M.V. (1998). *How to teach social skills*, 2nd edition. Austin, TX: Pro-Ed, Inc.

Paparozzi, M.A. & Gendreau, P. (2005). An intensive supervision program that worked: Service delivery, professional orientation, and organizational supportiveness. *The Prison Journal,* 85(4): 445-466.

Paparozzi, M. (1994). *An evaluation of the New Jersey board of parole's intensive supervision program.* Doctoral dissertation. Newark, NJ: Rutgers University.

Pearson, F.S., Lipton, D.S., Cleland, C.M., & Yee, D.S. (2002). The effects of behavioral/cognitive behavioral programs on recidivism. *Crime and Delinquency,* 48: 476-496.

Petersilia, J. (2000). *When prisoners return to the community: Political, economic, and social consequences.* Washington D.C.: National Institute of Justice, U.S. Department of Justice.

Petersilia, J. & Turner, S. (1993). Intensive probation and parole. In Michael Tonry (ed.), *Crime and justice: A review of research,* 17:281-335. Chicago: University of Chicago Press.

Petersilia, J. (1985). Probation and felony offenders. *Federal Probation,* 49: 4-9.

Prochaska, J. O., & DiClemente, C. C. (1983). Stages and processes of self-change of smoking: Toward an integrative model of change. Journal of Consulting and Clinical Psychology, 51, 390-395.

Prochaska, J.O. & Velicer, W.F. (1997). The transtheoretical model of health behavior change. *American Journal of Health Promotion,* 12(1): 38-48.

Prochaska, J.O., Redding, C. & Evers, K. (2008). The transtheoretical model and stages of change. In Karen Glanz, Barbara Rimer & K. Viswanath (Eds.), *Health education: Theory, research, and practice* 4th edition: 97 – 121. San Francisco, CA: Jossey-Bass A Wiley Imprint.

Robinson, C.R, VanBenshoten, S., Alexander, M., & Lowenkamp, C.T. (2011). A random (almost) study of staff training aimed at reducing rearrest (STARR): Reducing recidivism through intentional design. *Federal Probation,* 75(2): 57-63.

Rogers, C., (1961). *On becoming a person.* Boston: Houghton Mifflin.

Rooney, R.H. (1992). *Strategies for work with involuntary clients.* New York, NY: Columbia University Press.

Samenow, S. (1984). *Inside the criminal mind.* New York: Crown Publishers.

Serin, R., Mailloux, D., & Wilson, N. (2008). *Practice manual for use with the dynamic risk assessment for offender reentry (DRAOR).* Ottawa, ON: Carleton University.

Skeem, J., Eno Louden, J., Polasheck, & Cap, J. (2007). Relationship quality in mandated treatment: Blending care with control. *Psychological Assessment,* 19: 397-410.

Skinner, B. F. (1963). Operant behavior. *American Psychologist,* 18: 503-515.

Skinner, B.F. (1953). *Science and human behavior.* New York: Macmillan.

Smith, P., Lowenkamp, C.T., Latessa, E.J., Robinson, C.R. (2011). *New directions: Stopping domestic abuse.* Carson City, NV: The Change Companies.

Solomon, A., Kachnowski, V., & Bhati, A. (2005). *Does parole work? Analyzing the impact of postprison supervision on rearrest outcomes.* Washington, DC: The Urban Institute.

Spiegler, M. D., & Guevremont, D. C. (2003). *Contemporary behavior therapy* (4th ed.). Pacific Grove, CA: Wadsworth.

Spruance, L., Lowenkamp, C.T., and Latessa, E.J. (2005). *Changing offender behavior.* Carson City, NV: The Change Companies.

Striefel, S. (1998). *How to teach through modeling and imitation,* 2nd edition. Austin, TX: Pro-Ed, Inc.

Taxman, Faye (2002). Supervision—Exploring the dimensions of effectiveness. *Federal Probation* 66(2): 14-27.

Taxman, F.S. (2008). No illusion, offender and organizational change in Maryland's proactive community supervision model. *Criminology and Public Policy*, 7(2): 275-302.

The American Heritage® Stedman's Medical Dictionary. Retrieved February 11, 2011, from Dictionary.com website: http://dictionary.reference.com/browse/relationship

Thibadeau, S.F. (1998). How To Use Response Costs, 2nd edition. Austin, TX: Pro-Ed, Inc.

Thibadeau, S.F. (1998). *How to use response costs*, 2nd edition. Austin, TX: Pro-Ed, Inc.

Trotter, C. (1996) The impact of different supervision practices in community corrections. *Australian and New Zealand Journal of Criminology* 29(1): 29-46.

Trotter, C. (1999). *Working with involuntary clients: A guide to practice*. Thousand Oaks, CA: Sage Publications.

Van Houten, Ron (1998). *How to motivate others through feedback*, 2nd edition. Austin, TX: Pro-Ed, Inc.

Wilson, D. B., Bouffard, L. A. & Mackenzie, D. L. (2005). A quantitative review of structured, group-oriented, cognitive-behavioral programs for offenders. *Criminal Justice & Behavior*, 32: 172 – 204.

Wodahl, E.J., Garland, B., Culhane, S.E., & McCarty, W.P. (2011). Utilizing behavioral interventions to improve supervision outcomes in community-based corrections. *Criminal Justice & Behavior*, 38(4): 386-405.

Yochelson, S. & S. Samenow. (1977). *The criminal personality*, Volume 1. Chicago: Jason Aronson.

Yusuf, S., Hawken, S., Ounpuu, S., Dans, T., Avezum, A., Lanas, F., McQueen, M., Budaj, A., Pais, P., Varigos, J., Lisheng, L., on behalf of the INTERHEART Study Investigators. (2004). Effect of potentially modifiable risk factors associated with myocardial infarction in 52 countries (the INTERHEART study): case-control study. *Lancet* (364): 937-952.

APPENDIX

Figure A.1. Behavioral Analysis Worksheet

Behavioral Analysis

Think of the last ten times you got in trouble. Please list the details of those circumstances below. When you return to meet with your officer, you will review this worksheet to see if there are any patterns in your life that are leading you to "high-risk" situations for getting into trouble.

When (day of week and time)	Who were you with (before/during)?	Where were you?	What were you thinking/feeling (before/during)?	What did you do?	What were you thinking/feeling after?

When (day of week and time)	Who were you with (before/during)?	Where were you?	What were you thinking/feeling (before/during)?	What did you do?	What were you thinking/feeling after?

Figure A.2. Recognize, Avoid, Cope, Evaluate

RACE

(Material adapted from Spruance, Lowenkamp, and Latessa (2005). Carson City, NV: Change Companies)

This form is designed to help you keep track of situations (people, places, things) that increase your risk of getting into trouble. List the situations that you have recognized as being high-risk for you, how you plan to avoid them, if you can't avoid them how you will cope with them, and finally, how your avoidance and coping strategies have worked if you have tried them out. Think of ways you can improve your avoidance and coping skills each time you try one. Last, be sure to use self-reinforcement when you avoid or cope successfully!

Recognize Learn to recognize high-risk situations	**Avoid** Can you avoid? Plan to avoid	**Cope** If you cannot avoid, plan to manage	**Evaluate** How can you better handle the scenario? What did you do well?

AVOIDANCE WORKSHEET

My high risk PPTT is: _____. Can I realistically avoid it: _____

List all of the situations where you might encounter this PPTT (include specific places, triggers leading to):	If you avoid this situation what will you do instead (who will you hang out with, where will you go):	What specific steps will you take to avoid this situation (what will you say or do):	What problems do you anticipate in avoiding this situation:	What skills will you need to successfully implement the plan:

Coping Worksheet-Primary Plan

Complete the following worksheet to be used in situations where the high risk PPTT **CANNOT** be avoided. When encountering this high risk PPTT my risk reaction is: _____

List specific circumstances surrounding this PPTT that increase the likelihood of triggering your risk reaction:	What specific steps will you take to effectively cope with these circumstances:	What potential problems can you anticipate by implementing your plan:	How will you handle these problems:	What skills will you need to successfully implement the plan:

Coping Worksheet-Contingency Plan

Complete the following worksheet to be used in situations where the avoidance plan **has failed**

List some potential situations where the avoidance plan may fail:	What specific steps will you take to remove yourself with minimal risk of relapse or other problems:	What potential problems can you anticipate by implementing your plan:	How will you handle these problems:	What skills will you need to successfully implement the plan:

Figure A.3. Problem-Solving Worksheet

Problem-Solving Worksheet

Step 1. State the problem	
Step 2. Generate options	**Evaluate options**
Option 1.	Costs Benefits
Option2.	Costs Benefits
Option 3.	Costs Benefits
Option 4.	Costs Benefits
ADVANCED PLANNING Choose an option—I choose option #	
The steps I'll use to accomplish my plan are: 1. 2. 3. 4. 5. 6.	
Put the plan into action (who, what, when, where)	
I will use the plan in the following situations…. I will use the plan with the following people…. I will use the plan at the following times….	

Evaluate the plan
What went well? **Did I do all the steps?** **What was the outcome?** **Do I need more practice with the plan (role play)?** **Do I need a new plan?**

Figure A.4. Time-Out

Time-Out

(Skill adapted from Smith, Lowenkamp, Latessa, and Robinson (2011). Carson City, NV: Change Companies)
The Time-Out strategy is one you can begin using today, and is a skill to practice and continue to use as you work to make positive behavior change.

Taking a Time-Out can help you control your emotions and keep yourself and your partner safe. It involves removing yourself from a situation before losing control of your emotions and your anger.

Points of reference for using time-out

What to Do

1. Calmly tell your partner you are taking a Time-Out and that you will return or call when you have calmed down. Agree upon the amount of time beforehand. If you are not calm after the time has elapsed, let your partner know you need more time.

2. Leave the house. Do not just go to a different room.

3. Do not drive. Go for a walk or a run.

4. If you use a support person, make sure that it is someone who is prosocial. Do not contact a negative peer or past/potential romantic partner.

5. Do not use alcohol or other drugs.

6. Stay away long enough to regain control of your emotions. Your Time-Out should not last for several days or even overnight but, again, take as much time as you need until you feel in control of your emotions and behavior.

7. Call home to ensure that your partner is comfortable with your returning home before you do so.

8. Plan out, over the phone, what you will discuss and how you will resolve the conflict.

9. Remember that a Time-Out should NEVER be used as a way to win an argument. Do not use it as punishment over something that was said or as a control tactic.

Other Considerations

How do you know when you need to call a Time-Out? How do you know when you're losing control?

- When you experience physical signs (you feel your heart race or your face flush, you clench your jaw).
- When you begin to raise your voice and yell.
- When you start using threats or threatening behaviors.

You will want to talk to your partner about using Time-Outs *before* you are in a situation in which you need to use one.

Pick a time when you are both calm. Explain that you would like to try a new skill that might help both of you.

Then, discuss the guidelines for taking a time-out in the box on the previous page.

Figure A.5. Self-Assessment Form

Self-Assessment Form

Staff Member: _____ Offender: _____

Date: ____/____/____

Overall Skill Rating	Skill & Steps	Attempted	Comments
	Role Clarification		
	Identify agency goals		
	Ask for offender's goals		
	Identify officer's goals		
	Define supervision process		
	Confidentiality		
	Giving Feedback		
	Check if ready for feedback		
	Ask what they think they did well		
	Tell them what you think they did well		
	Ask what they might improve		
	Tell them discrepancies		
	Concrete examples		
	Check for understanding		
	Behavioral Analysis		
	Explain assignment		
	Review completion		
	Ask for their thoughts		
	Ask correct		
	Express concerns		
	Identify targets		
	RACE		
	Recognize		

Overall Skill Rating: 0 = No opportunity to use skill, 1 = Missed Opportunity, 2 = Used skill needs improvement, 3 = Proficient use of skill

Overall Skill Rating	Skill & Steps	Attempted	Comments
	Avoid		
	Cope		
	Reinforcement		
	Identify behavior		
	Discuss benefit		
	Offender ID Short term		
	Offender ID Long term		
	Contract future use		
	Disapproval		
	Identify behavior		
	Discuss costs		
	Offender ID Short term		
	Offender ID Long term		
	Offender ID Alternate		
	Contract future use		
	Authority		
	Focus on behavior		
	Calm voice		
	Choices and consequences		
	Encourage compliance		
	Praise compliance		
	Teach CM		
	Identify situation		
	Identify thoughts & replacement thoughts		
	Have offender apply		
	Contract for use		
	Review CM		
	Ask offender to ID situation		

Overall Skill Rating: 0 = No opportunity to use skill, 1 = Missed Opportunity, 2 = Used skill needs improvement, 3 = Proficient use of skill

Overall Skill Rating	Skill & Steps	Attempted	Comments
	Offender ID thoughts		
	Offender ID replacement thoughts		
	Offender describes consequence		
	Reinforce		
	Correct		
	Problem Solving		
	Stop, think, ID problem		
	Generate and evaluate solutions		
	Develop plan		
	Implement plan		
	Evaluate outcomes		

Overall Skill Rating: 0 = No opportunity to use skill, 1 = Missed Opportunity, 2 = Used skill needs improvement, 3 = Proficient use of skill

Figure A.6. Coaching Feedback Form

Coaching Feedback Form

Staff Member: _____   Peer Coach: _____
Offender: _____   Date: ____/____/____
Briefly describe the observed interaction:
_____
_____
_____
_____
_____

Overall Skill Rating	Skill & Steps	Attempted	Comments
	Role Clarification		
	Identify agency goals		
	Ask for offender's goals		
	Identify officer's goals		
	Define supervision process		
	Confidentiality		
	Giving Feedback		
	Check if ready for feedback		
	Ask what they think they did well		
	Tell them what you think they did well		
	Ask what they might improve		
	Tell them discrepancies		
	Concrete examples		
	Check for understanding		
	Behavioral Analysis		
	Explain assignment		
	Review completion		
	Ask for their thoughts		

Overall Skill Rating: 0 = No opportunity to use skill, 1 = Missed Opportunity, 2 = Used skill needs improvement, 3 = Proficient use of skill

Overall Skill Rating	Skill & Steps	Attempted	Comments
	Ask correct		
	Express concerns		
	Identify targets		
	RACE		
	Recognize		
	Avoid		
	Cope		
	Reinforcement		
	Identify behavior		
	Discuss benefit		
	Offender ID Short term		
	Offender ID Long term		
	Contract future use		
	Disapproval		
	Identify behavior		
	Discuss costs		
	Offender ID Short term		
	Offender ID Long term		
	Offender ID Alternate		
	Contract future use		
	Authority		
	Focus on behavior		
	Calm voice		
	Choices and consequences		
	Encourage compliance		
	Praise compliance		
	Teach CM		
	Identify situation		

Overall Skill Rating: 0 = No opportunity to use skill, 1 = Missed Opportunity, 2 = Used skill needs improvement, 3 = Proficient use of skill

Overall Skill Rating	Skill & Steps	Attempted	Comments
	Identify thoughts & replacements		
	Have offender apply		
	Contract for use		
	Review CM		
	Ask offender to ID situation		
	Offender ID thoughts		
	Offender ID replacement thoughts		
	Offender describes consequence		
	Reinforce		
	Correct		
	Problem Solving		
	Stop, think, ID problem		
	Generate and evaluate solutions		
	Develop plan		
	Implement plan		
	Evaluate outcomes		

Overall Skill Rating: 0 = No opportunity to use skill, 1 = Missed Opportunity, 2 = Used skill needs improvement, 3 = Proficient use of skill

Debrief

Did you ask team member if you could give feedback?   Yes   No

What did the team member identify as his or her strength(s) in the interaction?

What did the team member identify as his or her area(s) of improvement?

What did you see as his or her strength(s) in the interaction?

What did you see as an area of improvement in the interaction?

What behaviorally specific suggestions did you give the team member?

Figure A.7. Cognitive Model 1

Cognitive Model

EXTERNAL → **INTERNAL THOUGHTS** → **BEHAVIOR** → **CONSEQUENCES**

Figure A.8. Cognitive Model 2

Cognitive Model with Replacement Thoughts

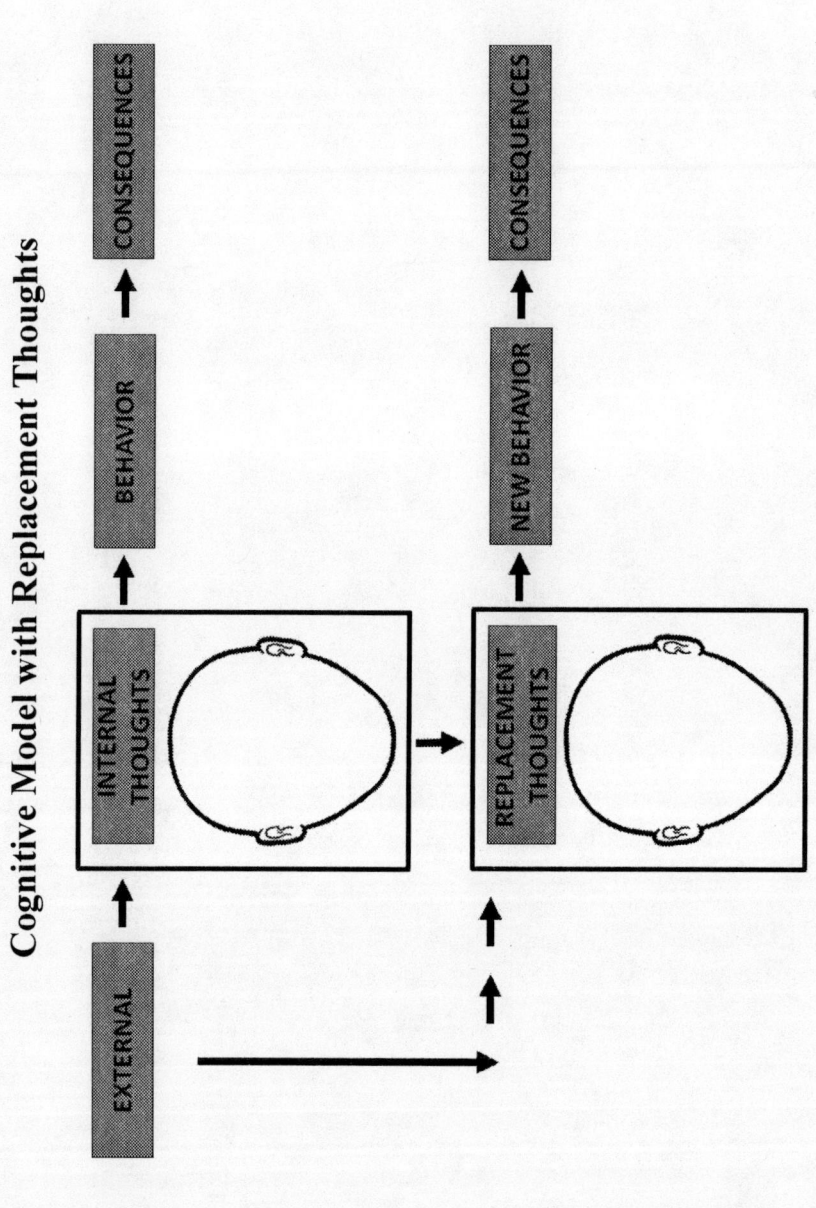